THE ATLANTIC CRITICAL REVIEW

QUARTERLY

A Peer Reviewed Journal Indexed in
MLA Directory of Periodicals

JULY – SEPTEMBER 2014

VOLUME 13 NUMBER 3

ATLANTIC
PUBLISHERS & DISTRIBUTORS (P) LTD

CONTRIBUTORS

Ajoy Sengupta, Assistant Professor of English, Asansol Girls' College, Asansol-4, Burdwan, West Bengal; [R] Shanti Apartment, Flat No. 3 / D [Opp. Indian Bank] Apcar Garden, Asansol-4, Dt, Burdwan, West Bengal.

Kamal Roy, Former Professor of English, North Bengal University, Ramkrishna Sarani, Shiv Mandir, North Bengal University, Raja Rammohunpur, Dt. Darjeeling, Siliguri, 734430, West Bengal.

Basavaraj Naikar, Former Professor Emeritus & Chairman, Department of English, Karnatak University, Dharwad 590003, Karnataka.

Shipra Gupta, M.Phil English, Utkal University, Bhubaneshwar, Odisha.

Rama Kundu, UGC Emeritus Fellow, Professor of English [Retired], Burdwan University, Burdwan-713104, West Bengal.

C. Sangluaii, Associate Professor and Head of Dept. (English), Govt. Serchhip College, Serchhip, Mizoram.

Jaswinder Singh, Research Scholar, Department of Humanities and Social Sciences, Indian Institute of Technology, Ropar, Punjab.

Rano Ringo, Assistant Professor, Department of Humanities and Social Sciences, Indian Institute of Technology, Ropar, Punjab.

Ritu Saluja, Assistant Professor, Delhi University, New Delhi.

THE ATLANTIC CRITICAL REVIEW
VOLUME 13 NUMBER 3 (JULY-SEPTEMBER 2014)

CONTENTS

The 'Other' Hardy

AJOY SENGUPTA

> O for a draught of vintage! that hath been
> Cool'd a long age in the deep-delvéd earth,
> Tasting of Flora and the country green,
> Dance, and Provençal song, and sunburnt mirth![1]

THOMAS Hardy (1840-1928), who is commonly known as a pessimistic writer standing on a 'Darkling Plain'[2] and supposed to be preoccupied with the seamy side of life, can be studied afresh from a comparatively unexplored perspective. Towards the end of his career Hardy expressed his dissatisfaction to W.W. Morgan complaining that his writings had not received 'fair reading' and 'fair judgement' (*Life* 402). The critics have generally emphasized his treatment of destiny, fate or chance, the circumscribing of free will, socio-economic infrastructure, and agony of industrialization or biological determinism. Indeed, "these different and at times conflicting approaches do not take into account the whole of Hardy. Thus, as one or other aspect is blown up, much remains unexplained or misinterpreted" (Kundu 1983, i). In Hardy there is not just one pattern; there are many patterns. Even within the space of a single novel of Hardy, one can trace various approaches which conflict yet cohere.

Furthermore, an in-depth study of his fiction manifests his fascination for another—a brighter—side of life as well. This is discernible in his portrayal of the rustic chorus, who on occasions show a gay abandon and an extraordinary hilarity. And sometimes, significantly enough, it is these jovial rustics who seem to steal the show. They prefer to indulge in a carefree, merry, and at times even exuberant response to the significant as well as to the comparatively unimportant events and issues of life around them. "Through the mirth of these people Hardy suggests, evokes and conjures up—though in a quite modified way—the old tradition of the mirth and the laughter of the carnivalesque, particularly the kind of drunken revelry that accounts for the special flavour of Rabelais's book."[3]

Throughout his career and particularly in his later years Hardy constantly resisted the label of a pessimist. He was considerably influenced by the Positivist Movement which was initiated in France by Saint Simon and later propagated by Comte. The movement entered England through Spencer, Huxley and Leslie Stephen. In the mid-1880s Hardy became a close companion of Frederic Harrison, the leader of the English positivists. *The Woodlanders* was also written and published during this period.

Hardy had been tremendously influenced by the new wave of ideas, generated by a host of literature including Darwin's *The Origin of Species*, and had already lost his faith in Christianity by the age of twenty-seven (Cecil 22). Inspired by the positivist ideas Hardy felt the necessity of a new religion and transposed his faith from the Almighty to human beings and the human society. Besides, he preferred to be considered a meliorist rather than a pessimist; he said, "On the contrary, my practical philosophy is distinctly meliorist" (Blunden 111). But what seems much more significant is the way Hardy endeavoured to recapture the folk-culture of England in some of his novels and stories, which had been rapidly vanishing from Wessex even during his lifetime (as mentioned in "The Dorsetshire Labourer"). "Humour is not the quality that one might expect to find in him [Hardy], so grand and so gloomy as he is", observes David Cecil, "but it is there all right. Nor is it incongruous with the rest of his achievement. It is rustic, it is elemental, it is grotesque, it is Gothic, it is traditional" (94). What D. Cecil does not mention is the 'carnivalesque' element that appears in some of Hardy's novels and stories. He captures the carnival ardour of the Wessex rustics to a significant extent in an entertaining way by incorporating the elements of unrestrained merriment like eating, drinking, gossiping, dancing and "sunburnt mirth of the rustic people who gladly scramble up the chariot of Bacchus whenever the situation permits".[4] Hardy can conjure up this spirit primarily because most of his novels and stories have country settings as their background which represents a waning past, and he focuses on such simple rustics who happen to be the traditional custodians and practitioners of the carnival jollity till the intrusion of industrialisation and subsequent urbanisation of spaces and people.

Hardy uses the carnivalesque in a chastened form as a way of reviving folk customs and folk life of the past. Categorising Hardy's characters into three different categories, J.C. Dave in *The Human Predicament in Hardy's Novels* places the rustics in the first category and observes, "Such rustics rarely get depressed, are easily consoled by the comforts of religion and recover fast from depression when occasionally they sink into it. They stand for the average humanity, unawakened to the plight of man in Nature, who toil with endurance through the dust and din of life enjoying the bliss of ignorance. They eat and drink and talk, without even a touch of melancholy" (30-31). Hardy himself observes, "It is among such communities as these that happiness will find her last refuge upon earth, since it is among them that a perfect insight into the conditions of existence will be longest postponed" (Orel 253).

The humour in the Wessex novels and stories is primarily rustic in nature as the author recaptures the tenor of joyous utterances and gestures of the villagers as they speak and perform. H.C. Duffin says, "Almost all the humour in the Wessex novels that is worth preserving is rustic humour—caught up with joy from the lips of the villagers themselves, redundancies removed, the form perfected, but otherwise the pure unadulterated essence of the South English peasantry of the third quarter of the nineteenth century" (144). The laughter, one expression of this humour, springs out of simple, genial enjoyment of life that the rustic people exhibit. It is neither satiric nor caustic and the author never ridicules the faults and follies of his rustic characters. David Cecil observes, "His are the jokes and anecdotes that enliven the evenings in cottage and village inn, and like theirs, his primary aim is simply to make us laugh. The mood which inspires them is simple, genial enjoyment—the countryman's slow relish of the absurd for its own sake. The main themes are the themes of most country humours—the naïve credulity of yokels and of crusted old eccentrics. We are made to laugh at the immemorial butts of village life—garrulous, reminiscent old grandfathers, henpecked husbands, ludicrous timid simpletons, and the incongruity between the facts of life and the countryman's ignorant comment on them" (94).

The rustics in Hardy's fiction, despite their tough and strenuous schedule, are endowed with such an irrepressible spirit that in a sense they emerge to be the happiest creations of Hardy. They are almost always in a jolly and buoyant mood, and are refreshingly entertaining with their rustic conversation and interaction. During carnivals or festivals, when they gather in an inn or under the open sky or around a bonfire, they enjoy food, drink, dance and music in the *carpe diem* spirit as they join these revelries. On such occasions they even dare to poke fun at the king or the church, and at death or marriage. Thus the hilarity of Hardy's rustics may well be placed in the proper carnival tradition of England.

Hardy's work is meticulously and essentially based on popular sources and thus it smacks of the ancient tradition of folk-humour. Carnival imparts his laughing chorus the stamina to enjoy in the face of day-to-day struggle and climactic events. Hardy's rustic people, with their rural idioms, sayings, proverbs, crude farces, display a kind of collective wisdom. They also manifest frank subversion of rank and authority. They not only fulfil the need of comic relief but with their formidable treasure of folk humour they offer a striking contrast to Hardy's melancholy and providence-stricken protagonists who are overwhelmed by life to suffer alone and perish alone.

The common folk in Hardy's fiction, unlike the serious characters of the front stage, appear to be fine illustrations of the Bakhtinian idea of revellers,—blasphemous rather than adoring, cunning rather than intelligent; coarse, dirty, physical, down-to-earth, revelling in drink, food and other bodily enjoyments. Thus they come to display the popular impulse of carnival.

Like the tipsy team of the 'Lord of Misrule'[5] the rustic community in Hardy's fiction performs the role of the laughing chorus of 'Carnival'. They seem to cater partially to the purpose of the intrinsic nature of the carnival laughter. Their gay laughter is generally festive and collective in nature. It belongs to all people, is directed at all and everyone including the participant. Basically it is gay and triumphant, sometimes mildly mocking and deriding too. This ambivalent laughter manifests the point of view of the entire community as well.

David Cecil identifies Hardy's chorus as

> the groups of rustics which in his greatest works form, as it were, the chorus to the main drama: the choir led by Tranter Dewey in "Under the Greenwood Tree"; the turf-cutters in "The Return of the Native"—Fairway, Christian, Grandfer Cantle and the rest; the cottagers of Little Hintock—Wood, Cawtree, Upjohn, Crendon; the Casterbridge gossips in "The Mayor of Casterbridge"; Bathsheba's labourers in "Far from the Madding Crowd"—Joseph Poorgrass, Henry Fray, Billy Smallbury, Jan Coggan; the grave-diggers in*A Pair of Blue Eyes*; Haymoss, Blore and the rest of Lady Constantine's tenantry in "Two on a Tower". They cannot be compared with the

> central figures in the drama just because they are placed in a story to provide a chorus. (91-92)

It is noteworthy that Hardy's rustics always appear in a group and rarely as individuals. Their characters are never full-length delineations. Cecil has tried to place them in the Shakespearean tradition. These characters, according to Cecil, "are the direct descendants of Bottom and Dogberry and the rustics who gather in response to Falstaff's call to arms at the house of Justice Shallow [...]. Rich fragments of rusticity, they are as entertaining as any of the classic comic characters of Fielding and Goldsmith. But unlike theirs and like Shakespeare's, they can also stir serious emotions" (92).

Hardy portrays the festive life of people which is, *à la* Bakhtin, their second life,—organized on the basis of laughter. Bakhtin believes that folk custom is the origin of the carnivalesque which was a way to overcome apprehension of the king, the church, the hell, the plague, and the serious. Hardy uses the carnivalesque in a modified and chastened manner as a part of his revival of the folk tradition of the past. At the same time Hardy's rustics manifest a carnivalesque approach of defying terrestrial and ethereal fears through laughter.

The rustic chorus hardly indulge in parodic laughter. However, they illustrate that "carnival achieves a transformation downward or 'uncrowning' *de jure* relations of dependency, expropriation, and social discipline" (Bristol 22); they, on the occasions of their carnival revelry, indulge in irreverence, cursing, obscene hints, as also in dance, music, feasting and drinking. By their hilarious enjoyment they consistently endeavour to offer the possibility of interpreting life from another perspective than the serious and sombre one. This festive mirth indeed constitutes a common feature of Hardy's works. The simple parties in rustic households, especially, on winter evenings, are occasions for uninhibited mirth and revelry in Hardy's novels. As Cecil remarks,

> Hardy's descriptions of dancing are especially memorable—he loved it himself as a young man. To the end of his life the names of the old dance-tunes—"The Lady's Triumph", "The Dashing White Sergeant"—struck a wistful, responsive chord in his heart. They were not the languid unsociable peregrination of the modern dance, but the old country dances, festive, communal and energetic, all leaps and twirls and linked hands. They went on and on, until the chalk

> rose in clouds from the floor and the sweat shone on the dancers' foreheads. (106)

Hardy's humour is often verbal in nature depending for its impact on the particular words used by the author. The intrinsic poetic quality in him is delightfully manifested in the speech of the rustics. This humour has also an Elizabethan fervour in its leisurely flourish of whimsical fancy. The Elizabethan bias for the macabre (the Hamletian grave-diggers, for instance) is expressed through his sense of the irony of human destiny which is sometimes displayed by a hearty fun related to coffins and funerals:

> Ah, poor lord George! he [Martin Cannister, a mason] continued, looking contemplatively at the huge coffin; he and I was as bitter enemies once as any could be when one is a lord and t' other only a mortal man. [...] But once now and then when I looked at his towering height, I'd think in my inside, "What a weight you'll be, my lord, for our arms to lower under the aisle of Endelstow Church some day!" [*A Pair of Blue Eyes* 200]

Solomon Longways' comment—"Why should death rob life o' fourpence. I say there was no treason in it." [*The Mayor of Casterbridge* 126]—reverberates with echoes from a long tradition; one is reminded Dame Quickly's account of Falstaff's death [in Shakespeare's *King Henry IV*]. There is a universality and timeless proverbial feature about this ordinary utterance. "We forget Solomon Longways", observes Cecil, "and seem to be listening to the voice of all humble humanity as, from the wisdom of its hard workaday experience, it makes unillusioned its comment on the mystery of death" (93). Hardy's rustics manifest the quality of defying the annihilating power of death and like people in the carnivalesque tradition they seem to realize and assert the inherent implication of the cycle of rebirth and regeneration. While contrasting between the novels of Dostoevsky and Tolstoy in *Problems of Dostoevsky's Poetics* (1929), Bakhtin argues that the former's novels are in the 'dialogic' or 'polyphonic' form, where the characters are allowed to speak in their own voices. They are liberated to speak "a plurality of independent and unmerged voices of consciousness, a genuine polyphony of fully valid voices..." (Cuddon 219). In Hardy we note this plurality; besides the voice of the so-called 'tragic protagonists', there is a clearly audible voice of the laughing people in his novels. The elements of mirth in the festivities are the secret of their strength and sustenance. The rustic bystanders prove that life can be endured and even enjoyed when approached from another point of view. They manifest that despite the everyday material struggle, it is still possible to laugh out the problems of life. Although individuals suffer, the Wessex folk enjoy themselves in spite of the strains of life.

The rustics thus serve to provide a counterpoint to Hardy's main plots. They represent the vast majority of humdrum herd, who continue living their unruffled life, whatever catastrophe may overwhelm the protagonists: "Henchard and Eustacia may love and suffer and die; but the rustics go on. It is they who bring the children to birth, dance at the wedding, mourn at the graveyard, and speak the epitaph over the tomb. They are eternal as the earth by which they live. And their very prosaicness anchors the story to reality. It gives the reader a standard of normality by which he can gauge the tremendous heights and depths to which the main characters rise and fall" (Cecil 93-94).

The carnivalesque impulse can be traced through the Hardy canon right from *Under the Greenwood Tree* till *The Woodlanders*; however this charming rustic band, disappears in his final novels. This decline in the elements of laughter can be partly explained by the unhappiness in the author's own conjugal life; but a profounder reason can be traced in his essay "The Dorsetshire Labourer" (July 1883) [*Longman's Magazine*, 252-69]. In this essay Hardy notes in a melancholy mood how, as a result of annual migration "the humorous simplicity that formerly characterized the men and the unsophisticated modesty of the women are rapidly disappearing or lessening, under the constant attrition of lives mildly approximating to those of workers in a manufacturing town" (Orel 180).

Bakhtin observes, "To ignore or to underestimate the laughing people of the Middle Ages also distorts the picture of European culture's historic development" (6). Hardy presents the progeny, a little enfeebled and chastened though, of those ancient generations of laughing people of the rural England. He never ignores or underestimates the laughing rustics of Wessex who contributed to a significant extent to constitute the history of the local culture. He argues in the essay: "the pleasures enjoyed by the Dorset labourer may be far from pleasures of the highest kind desirable for him. They may be pleasures of the wrong shade. And the inevitable glooms of a straitened hard-working life occasionally enwrap him from such pleasures as he has; and in times of special storm and stress the 'Complaint of Piers the Ploughman' is still echoed in his heart. But even

Piers had his flights of merriment and humour; and ploughman as a rule do not give sufficient thought to the morrow to be miserable when not in physical pain" (Orel 171). In the same essay Hardy reacted against the contemporary practice of projecting the rustics as the melancholy, dull, comical 'Hodge': "The happiness of a class can rarely be estimated aright by philosophers who look down upon that class from the Olympian heights of society" (Orel 172).

The present work attempts to consider Hardy's novels and short stories in the light of the carnivalesque which is, of course, much less robust here than their Rabelaisian manifestations. However, I have endeavoured to show the sunny side of the oeuvre of Hardy's major fiction though he is usually perceived as a pessimistic writer. The elements of laughter are never scanty in his earlier novels; and from *Under the Greenwood Tree* (his second novel) to *The Woodlanders* (his eleventh novel) they are incorporated by the author as necessary components of his design. Some of his short stories also abound with these elements. An intensive textual analysis has been attempted in the following chapters and the texts are allowed to speak for themselves.

To set my work in perspective I have tried to present in "The Premise" (Chapter 1), the position accorded to laughter in the social life and literary arena of England and Europe through the ages. The chapter also endeavours to take into account some of the conventional approaches regarding the presence of the elements of laughter in literary works. It also attempts to identify the presence of the carnivalesque in British Literature, which may help us to see if we can place Hardy's rustics in the age-old carnival tradition of England.

The second chapter explores the carnivalesque elements in *Under the Greenwood Tree*. This novel of Hardy introduces abundant merriment, laughter and festivity. It illustrates the author's optimistic outlook and ends in fulfilment. The Mellstock Quire is a fictional name for the Stinsford choir with which Hardy had long family association. The novel is based on the materials which have been adapted from the author's first-hand experience or anecdotes listened to in his young age. This work portrays the jovial rustics of Mellstock epitomizing the continuation of the carnival spirit even in the nineteenth-century England.

An intensive study of *A Pair of Blue Eyes* is made in Chapter 3 to highlight the 'decrowning' of nobility, church and death in the novel. This first novel of Hardy to be published with the author's name on the title page is reminiscent of his first meeting with Emma, his first wife. This work portrays the simple genial humour of the country life, the rural customs, beliefs and the rustic's ability to revel on festive occasions despite their strenuous everyday schedule.

The spirit that in spite of regular material strain and struggle makes it possible for one to laugh out the problems of life is manifested in *Far from the Madding Crowd*, the novel which is analysed in the fourth chapter. This novel reverberates with the uproarious voice of the common people beside the sad serious voice of the so-called 'tragic protagonists'. This work in which the author first uses the fictional name 'Wessex', is a rural painting of the simple folk of the south-western counties of England in their boozing and rejoicing which provides the tragic texture of the novel with comic relief.

The fifth chapter examines *The Return of the Native* to bring out the latent carnival spirit which still existed in rural England of the time though it had already disappeared from the upper strata of the society. It brings out the elements of laughter in the people's mass indulgence in riotous dance and music, consumption of victuals and liquor, as well as the inversion of social hierarchies. Extensive participation of the rustics on the occasions like Maypole celebration exemplifies the continuing presence of the carnival ardour even in the nineteenth century.

The sixth chapter explores *The Trumpet-Major* to show the continuation of the *carpe diem* spirit even at a moment of national crisis. Written with the local history of Dorset and Weymouth during the Napoleonic invasion as the backdrop, this novel displays Rabelaisian mirth. At a time of concern and tension, the commoners manifest their zest for delight and entertainment. Counted as the "lightest-hearted novel Hardy ever wrote" (Duffin 22), this novel portrays the rustic community indulging in carnival jocundity.

Through a scrutiny of *The Mayor of Casterbridge* in the seventh chapter I have tried to trace the carnivalesque even in this tragic novel. Even here the semi-urban ambience presents adequate evidence of the common people's jovial disposition. 'Uncrowning' death and celebration of life in the face of imminent death, which undoubtedly suggest carnival temperament, are displayed by characters like Christopher Coney who manifest the Bacchanalian spirit. Besides, the plebeians illustrate the craving for 'decrowning' their social superiors, as well as for drinking, eating and collective revelry.

The Woodlanders which may be said to be Hardy's last novel with ample evidences of carnival attitude is analysed in the eighth chapter. The rustic bystanders of Little Hintock evince extraordinary hilarity despite the moments of pathos in the lives of the protagonists. Living close to nature and being soaked in the tradition of their primitive ancestors, they are imbued with a freshness and fellow-feeling. With their genial disposition they enjoy feasting, gossiping, playing cards or musical instruments—of course along with drenching their throats with liquor. Despite their hard labour in bark-ripping they remain hale and hearty in their 'appreciative throats'.

The ninth chapter explores the thin trickle of laughter flowing through Hardy's novels other than those analysed in the preceding chapters.

Most of Hardy's short stories, unlike his novels, are vibrant with the robust vigour of the rustics. The tenth chapter examines some selected stories in which is depicted by the author reminisces the anecdotes, legends and chronicles of the local history. While shunning the tragic vision of Von Hertmann and Schopenhauer, in many of these stories Hardy presents the exuberant laughter of the simple folk. Some of these short stories resemble the traditional English ballad.

The inferences drawn from the probing in these ten chapters are summed up in the concluding chapter.

This work, thus, proposes to explore some of the features of Hardy's novels and short stories which have received comparatively less critical attention. It endeavours to re-read the so-called 'pessimistic' writer in order to bring out the 'other' side of his work which foregrounds elements of laughter and merriment.

NOTES

1. John Keats, *Ode to a Nightingale*, 11-14.
2. The title of H.C. Webster's book on Hardy. According to Webster, Hardy's philosophy 'as a whole may be called either deterministic or fatalistic' (156).
3. Kundu, R. "Charioted by Bacchus: 'The Lord of Misrule' and the Carnivalesque in Hardy's Stories" published in *Atlantic Critical Review*, Vol. 1, No. 2, Oct-Dec, 2002: 76.

   Hardy attended the Rabelais Club in London in 1879, 1883 and 1886. This information is furnished in F.E. Hardy's book *The Life of Thomas Hardy*.
4. Kundu, R. *Atlantic Critical Review*, 78.

5. A holiday custom prevalent in some parts of Europe. C.L. Barber in *Shakespeare's Festive Comedy* informs that in this custom "the rougher pleasures of defiance and mockery are uppermost, [...] Abuse predominates [...]. The formal Lord of Misrule presided over the eating and drinking within-doors in the cold season. But the title was also applied to the captain of summer Sunday drinking and dancing by the young men of a parish [...]" (24).

(A) WORKS BY THOMAS HARDY

Under the Greenwood Tree. Hertfordshire: Wordsworth Editions, 1994.

A Pair of Blue Eyes. Hertfordshire: Wordsworth Editions, 1995.

Far from the Madding Crowd. Hertfordshire: Wordsworth Editions, 1993.

The Return of the Native. New York: W.W. Norton & Co., 1969.

The Trumpet Major. London: Penguin Books, 1996.

The Mayor of Casterbridge. Madras: Oxford UP, 1989.

The Woodlanders. Hertfordshire: Wordsworth Editions, 1996.

(B) WORKS ON THOMAS HARDY

Blunden, Edmund. *Thomas Hardy*. London: Macmillan, 1962.

Cecil, David. *Hardy: The Novelist*. Ludhiana: Lyall Book Depot, 1967.

Dave, Jagadish Chandra. *The Human Predicament In Hardy's Novel*. London: Macmillan, 1985.

Duffin, H.C. *Thomas Hardy*. London: Oxford UP, 1993.

Hardy, F.E. *The Life of Thomas Hardy* (1840-1928) London: Macmillan, 1970.

(C) OTHER WORKS

Bristol, Michael D. *Carnival and Theater: Plebian Culture and the Structure of Authority in Renaissance England*. New York: Methuen, 1985.

Cuddon, J.A. *A Dictionary of Literary Terms and Literary Theory*. New Delhi: Blackwell, 1998.

❑❑❑

W. Somerset Maugham: The Man and the Writer: A New Perspective

KAMAL ROY

> Nothing is consistent, nothing is fixed or certain in my life. By turns I resemble and differ, there is no living creature so foreign to me that I cannot be sure of approaching.—Andre Gide, *Journals 1889—1949*

> […] man never has lived and cannot live without a philosophy of life.—Leo Tolstoy, *A Confession, The Gospel in Brief and What I Believe*

> Faith in reason is the trust that the ultimate natures of things lie together in a harmony which excludes mere arbitrariness.—A.N. Whitehead, *Science and the Modern World*

> […] the more perfect the artist, the more completely separate in him will be the man who suffers and the mind which creates; the more perfectly will be the mind digest and transmute the passions which are its material.—T.S. Eliot, *The Sacred Wood*

EVERY creative person is, according to Jung, *per se* a divided being; he is at once "a human being with a personal life" and "an impersonal creative process" (*Modern Man* 194). What, however, is peculiar to Maugham is that it is not the exigencies of art but the wounds of life that fracture his self. There is an almost critical consensus that the orphan Maugham is a classic instance of the deprived child. Morgan very aptly calls the trauma of his mother's death to the boy Maugham his "original wound" (9), Calder equally aptly "a devastation" (*Willie* 8). Morgan then suggests "a connection between Maugham's decision to be a writer and the death of his mother" (45), Calder between "the death of Edith Maugham" and "Maugham's homosexual temperament" (*Willie* 11). The psychiatrist Laing thinks that "loss of the mother, at a certain stage, threatens the individual with loss of his self" (*Divided Self* 116). Maugham too holds that the death of his mother has caused him a permanent wound. Such has been its cumulative effect that "I have never quite lost the sense that my living life was a mirage in which I did this and that because that was how it fell out, but which, even while I was playing my part in it, I could look at from a distance and know for the mirage it was" (*Summing Up* 182). The mother's traumatic death that disintegrates his self and derealizes his life most likely orientates him in course of time towards mysticism as well. Be that as it may, the sudden transfer of the hitherto cosseted boy from the cosmopolitan, luxurious, loving ambience of his parental home in Paris to that of the provincial, unloving vicarage of his stern uncle in Whitstable must have simply unhinged him. Exposed as he is to life's grim reality, and that too in his most impressionable years, he has every reason to look upon himself as fate's chosen victim. No less damaging is his boyhood bilingualism. The mature Maugham is not exactly the average Englishman. It is all because of his birth in France which has "enabled me to learn French and English simultaneously and thus instilled into me two modes of life, two liberties, two points of view" (*Selected Prefaces* 79). This doubleness has prevented him from developing a strong sense of belonging and hence a secure sense of self-identity. His stammer too has affected his overall personality. A bar to easy and spontaneous communication with his fellows and a cause of humiliation, it turns him into a shy, self-conscious introvert.

The first climacteric of Maugham's youth is his loss of faith during his heuristic pilgrimage in Germany (1890-92). His intellect cocks a snook at God; his instinct cowers at the thought of the Devil. The long-term effect of his instinct-intellect polarity is that his determined effort to resolve it generates the spiritual dynamic that sustains his creativity for over five decades. Nevertheless a note of wistfulness marks his confession on the issue: "It may be that my heart, having found rest nowhere, had some deep ancestral craving for God and immortality which my reason would have no truck with" (*SU* 182). To return after this brief excursus to the immediate effect of Maugham's psychic split. Unsurprisingly the twenty-two-year-old Maugham's multiple personality precipitates his identity crisis, tellingly captured in one of the few giveaways in *A Writer's Notebook*: "There are times when I look over the various parts of my character with perplexity. I recognize that I am made up of several persons and that the person which at the moment has the upper hand will inevitably give place to another. But which is the real me? All of them or none" (17)? Maugham's relentless search for the authentic self has thus a personal urgency behind it. A plausible answer to Maugham's anxious query is that his very awareness of his several fragmentary, fleeting selves argues the existence of a focal self, implicated in and yet transcendent to them all. Maugham's split self, however, can both amuse and anguish him. The young Maugham's puckish self makes fun of his meditative self's preoccupation with such metaphysical issues as life's meaningfulness or otherwise and God's existence or nonexistence: "He raged, a twopenny-halfpenny Prometheus, as unquiet thoughts gnawed at his heart, while he strove to pierce the mystery of life" (*WN* 56). This capacity of Maugham to look at himself from the outside is the source of his humour and of his tolerance.

Maybe Maugham's polarity spawns some of his quirks such as his flair for clinical self-scrutiny. It is shown at its best when, with his characteristic cool, he registers the minutiae of what may have been his last moment. As the victim of a boat accident, Maugham was trying desperately to keep afloat: "I suppose the struggle was so severe that there was no time for any emotion, and even when I felt my strength going and thought that in a moment or two I should have to give up, I am not conscious that I had any feeling of fear or even distress at the thought of death by drowning" (*WN* 163). This tendency on Maugham's part to split himself into subject and object and to deploy the one to anatomize the other may erode spontaneity, but it certainly conduces to insight. It is by exploiting his duality that Maugham has "caught anything of the precious quality in circumstances which in others would have seemed to me instinct with its fine flower" (*Chinese Screen* 59). An intensely private person, Maugham confesses to being by nature both suspicious and secretive. No wonder his own nephew and a homosexual writer at that, Robin Maugham avers that "I never understood him" (213). His further claim that very few of Maugham's friends ever pierced the layers of morbid shyness caused by the misery of his youth is borne out by Noel Coward, another homosexual writer. Coward, indebted to Maugham "for nearly fifty years of kindness and hospitality", admits that "I cannot truthfully say that I really knew him intimately" (Foreword to Garson Kanin's *Remembering Maugham* n. pg). As an analyst of his own life and personality, barring of course his tabooed homosexuality, Maugham outrivals his biographers. It redounds to his candour to admit unflinchingly that "I am either too self-centred, or too diffident, or too reserved, or too shy to be able to be on confidential terms with anyone I know at all well" (*Vagrant Mood* 196). Given to peering into the depths of other selves as much as into his own, Maugham delights in exposing "the discrepancies of human nature" and "the disparity between appearance and reality". Humour, he insists, teaches tolerance. The humorist understands and so forgives (*SU* 39-40). The least censorious of writers, Maugham can with remarkable ease slip into the skin of characters of all shades, and think their thoughts and feel their feelings. Even his worst detractors concede him unusual powers of observation, though they mistake his tolerance for his amorality. It is to his multiple personality, the source of his insight and of his sympathy, that Maugham owes his success in creating a host of living characters. Naturally the writer, as Maugham conceives him, "is not one man but many. It is because he is many that he can create many and the measure of his greatness is the number of selves that he comprises" (*SU* 135).

Maugham's proffered reasons for not being "a social person" range from his lack of "facility for games", his inhibitive stammer, his "instinctive shrinking from my fellow men" to his incapacity to "forget myself". A compulsive loner, he always returns from his occasional spells of globe-trotting and socialities "to my books and my company with relief" (*SU* 53). As is his practice, Maugham transfers his own character trait to the artist. Accordingly he concludes that the artist is "a lone wolf. His way is solitary" (*WN* 267). The solitary Maugham is literally a book addict. He retreats into the haven of books from life's stress and strain. He also engages in the exploration of the great literature of the past just to enrich his self. If he has not "felt some of the fundamental emotions of normal men" (*SU* 46), it is more likely because he is a self-divided introvert than because he is a homosexual. In any case, Maugham's artist partakes of life only with part of him. He never feels "the common emotions of men with his whole being, for...he is an observer as well as an actor" (*SU* 136).

Antinomic to the very core of his being, Maugham keeps on swinging from one pole of his personality to the other. His one ambition is to become a successful writer, his other to become a whole man. He courts life experience for professional reasons; he also savours it for its own sake. That is why he is determined to live a rich, variegated private life as a man of the world (*SU* 53). Intent on living life to the full, he accords equal importance to flesh and spirit. Evidently he lives out to perfection his idea of the writer who seeks "to prevent himself from becoming one-sided. He never gets the opportunity to grow into a self-consistent coherent creature" (*SU* 135). His one self hungers for life; his other recoils from it. Maugham the worldling has his contrary in Maugham the recluse. He feels more at home only in his own company. There is, however, a third Maugham, haunted by a mystic vision that beckons him on to a supernal city. The city he sees in his sleep leaves him a trifle puzzled because

> I know vaguely what the men are in those cities of mystics, the manner of them and the peace they offer to the tortured heart; but what kind of men they are in this city of mine and why it is that all those others on the road so passionately seek it, I do not know. I only know that it imports me urgently to go there, and that when at last I slip through its gates, happiness awaits me. (*WN* 191)

Maugham's existential and creative contradictions intermingle. Morgan has sampled some of them with all their paradoxical flavour: his profound love for his mother contrasts with his low opinion of women; his married state with his homosexuality; his low opinion of the human species with his high tolerance of human frailty (615). As the prince of antinomies, Maugham, as cameoed above, approximates to Laing's image of a "schizoid":

> Such a person is not able to experience himself 'together with' others or 'at home in' the world, but, on the contrary, he experiences himself in despairing aloneness and isolation; moreover, he does not experience himself as a complete person but rather as 'split' in various ways, perhaps as a mind more or less tenuously linked to a body, as two or more selves, and so on. (*Divided Self* 17)

The novelist Maugham too has his fair share of contradictions no less glaring. He declares, as a starter, to be "devoid of the pedagogic interest" (*SU* 7), to "have always eschewed the prophetic role" (*SU* 84) and to "have never been a propagandist" (*SU* 127). Quite consistent with these disclaimers is his habitually modest claim that "I have had some story to tell and it has interested me to tell it. To me it has been a sufficient object in itself" (*SU* 130). In pointed contrast to this, however, is his counterclaim that "there is no such thing as a 'mere' story". When he writes a story, the author [...], willy-nilly offers a criticism of life" (*Points of View* 174). This volte-face extends to the novelist as well. Accordingly Maugham asserts that "to describe a novelist as a mere storyteller is to dismiss him with contumely", and that "there is no such creature". Since the novelist offers "a criticism of life", he is, concludes Maugham, very much "a moralist" (*Ten Novels* 19). Contradictions would seem, on his own testimony, to have marked his actual practice of novel-writing. "I have always worked", generalizes Maugham, "from the living model" (*SU* 40). But he seems to recommend the converse as a better option: "Biographies and reminiscences, technical works, will give you often an intimate detail, a telling touch, a revealing hint, that you might never have got from a living model" (*SU* 55). Maugham does not approve of the "writers who claim from thc rcadcr an cffort to understand their meaning" (*SU* 18). Still he enjoins the novelist "to prevent the reader from finding him out" (*Writer's Point of View* 13) and the writer not to "explain over-much" (*WN* 276). He ends up by envisaging the reader as a coauthor since "you only get out of a book what you put into it and you see in it only what you are" (*WN* 279). And now comes the crowning conundrum: "Unless a novelist makes you believe in him he is done, and yet if he is entirely believable he may very well be dull" (*WN* 257).

To extricate Maugham from the veritable thicket of confusion as presented above, what needs to be spelt out is the kind of novelist he is. As a neophyte writer, the twenty-two-year-old Maugham records in his *Writer's Notebook* under the year 1896 what is virtually his literary manifesto: "My object is to find a rule of conduct for the average man under the normal conditions of the present day" (23). First he tentatively suggests an intimate relation between literature and morals: "The history of human morals is very well brought to light in the course of literature: the writer, with whatever subject he deals, displays the code of morals of his own age" (*WN* 14). Later he emphatically declares that the artist "creates his own values" (*SU* 112). Granted that every artist is as a matter of course a moralist, even then the young Maugham's ethical project carries about it an aura of special urgency, for his recent apostasy requires him to find out a viable substitute. The extent of his ethical obsession is evident from his self-portrait at the age of twenty-two:

> I wander about alone, forever asking myself the same questions: What is the meaning of life? Has it any object or end? Is there such a thing as morality? How ought one to conduct himself in life? What guide is there? Is there one road better than another? And a hundred more of the same sort. (*WN* 26)

To conduct his value quest with a semblance of competence requires a thorough grounding in philosophy. Fortunately Maugham has the required philosophical bent of mind.

Such is the young Maugham's intellectual sensitivity that "A fresh idea dawns upon me and I feel myself uplifted from the workaday world to the blue empyrean of the spirit" (*WN* 17). Ideas mean so much to him that he gets into the habit of starting "the day with a perusal of a few pages of a metaphysical work" (*Gentleman in the Parlour* 100). His occasional holidays from his otherwise strict writing schedule do not, however, interrupt his compulsive philosophical studies. He goes, for instance, on his long Malaya journey, armed with a copy of Bradley's *Appearance and Reality* (*Gentleman* 101) and with the intention of reaching some conclusions about "errors and evil, space, time, chance and mutability" (*Gentleman* 34). This enthusiasm for philosophy, evident from his teens, survives well into his seventies. He records on his seventieth birthday that everything he once held dear has receded into irrelevance except "one subject with which I can still occupy myself with my old excitement, and that is philosophy" (*WN* 286).

The young Maugham sets about readying himself for his ethical undertaking with zeal and discipline. Initiated in his teens into the charm of philosophy by Kuno Fischer at Heidelberg, he moves from the exploration of both ancient and modern philosophical classics to the systematic study of "Ethics" (*SU* 148) and then of "epistemology" (*SU* 153). Such is his passion for "metaphysics" (*WN* 122) that he extols it as irresistible and inexhaustible, great and uplifting, inspiring and consoling. Treating as it does of the universe, of God and immortality, of the nature of reason and purpose of life (*SU* 141), metaphysics must have, to enthuse him so much, touched a sensitive chord in his being. Presumably though his projected philosophical treatise aborts, his metaphysical passion remains unabated. The assumption that Maugham's philosophical preoccupations permeate his novels too will be subsequently documented. To proceed now with Maugham's idea of the desiderated "good novel" which has no room for any issues that are purely local and ephemeral. It should have "a widely interesting theme" and "of enduring interest" (*Ten Novels* 14). Thus circumscribed, it can stake only "the great issues of life" out as its province. "The novelist has the right", Maugham explicitly claims, "to deal with those great topics which are of concern to every human being, the existence of God, the immortality of the soul, the meaning and value of life" (*Ten Novels* 15-16). Maugham thus turns the novelist for all practical purposes into a surrogate metaphysician. His own mature novels from *Of Human Bondage* onwards are metaphysical and mystical in nature.

More than a devoted student of philosophy, Maugham is also an eclectic system-builder. It is as an eighteen-year-old atheist medical student that he entered in the autumn of 1892 the world of late-nineteenth-century science, dominated by materialism. The tyro's reaction to science, not as a mass of disconnected information but as a set of ideas, underlines his propensity for systematic thinking. The first ever "rule of conduct" he formulates on the basis of his growing "familiarity with certain principles" (*SU* 42) is of course a materialist one. A system with the youthful Maugham, however, is not a straitjacket but a springboard. An entry in *A Writer's Notebook* under the year 1896 shows him engaged in hammering out a second system:

> Now after nearly two years in which I have occupied myself in looking for some rule, in which I have asked myself what is the reason, the aim, the object of life, I just begin to have a vague notion of what I take to be the truth. Answers to all these questions are slowly forming themselves in my mind; but at present everything is confused. I have collected a mass of facts, ideas, experience, but I cannot yet arrange them into any system or order them in a definite pattern. (*WN* 25)

Evidently it is not a ragbag but a systematic philosophy that he is after. What was still inchoate in 1896 crystallizes out two years later. Accordingly Maugham claims that "By the time I was twenty-four I had constructed a complete system of philosophy. It rested on two principles: The Relativity of Things and the Circumferentiality of Man" (*SU* 148). What keeps on changing is Maugham's intellectual position but not his passion for a system. As he progresses from subjective to absolute idealism, he leaves behind the idea of man as a self-enclosed monad for the idea of man as an integral part of the cosmos as such. He further envisages the entire universe as a system of interlocking events where everything "combines to cause every one of our actions" (*SU* 166). This belief in the interconnectedness of things marks Maugham out as a monist. For the monists, explains Ewing,

> have commonly thought that two different things could only be related if they formed a unity so that they could not ultimately be

> separated.[…] Some have inferred that, since everything is related in some way to everything else, the universe as it stands must be regarded as a very closely knit unity. (*Fundamental Questions* 209)

Maugham's empirical streak serves as a brake on the idealist's potential excesses, and keeps his feet firmly on the ground. He gathers various ideas, but accepts only those that pass the test of his lived experience and of his knowledge of the world. His successive systems reflect his ever widening and deepening vision. They grow one out of the other in a process of progressive refinement and comprehensiveness. Their shared nucleus, however, is his settled belief in anti-intellectualism which also informs his contemplated philosophical project. His gleanings for this treatise

> satisfied not only my mind but, what I could not but think more important than my mind, the whole body of my instincts, feelings and deep-rooted prejudices, the prejudices that are so intimate a part of one that they can hardly be distinguished from instincts; and out of them make a system that would be valid for me and enable me to pursue the course of my life. (*SU* 151)

As his monism, so Maugham's holism perfectly coordinates with absolute idealism, which pivots on the "conception of an *organic whole*" and predicates "the ethical criterion" on "life as a whole" (Ewing, *Idealism* 430). With oneness or unity as his consuming passion, Maugham naturally looks "for a system of philosophy as coherent and self-contained as Bradley's, in which one part hung necessarily on another" (*SU* 151). Maugham gives up for lack of time the plan of writing out his projected philosophical treatise. Ivor Brown mistakenly thinks that "Maugham abandoned his attempt to formulate a philosophical system that would be valid for him and enable him to pursue the course of his life with clearly defined principles" (25).

Maugham's passion for "system" in philosophy has its exact parallels in his similar passion for "pattern" in life and "form" in art. A natural sense of tidiness has prompted him even in his very youth to design a pattern for his life (*SU* 30). Since "I have gone my way, following the course I had mapped out for myself, and trying with my works to fill out the pattern I looked for" (*SU* 132), the pattern of his life and of his art is substantially the same. The creation of his life-pattern, however, requires a good deal of intellectual scouting. As a matter of fact, it demands cogent answers to some of the fundamental questions of philosophy.

Hence his arduous philosophical preparation. He rightly stresses the philosophical underpinnings of his life-pattern. It requires him to know something about the general structure of the universe, whether there is an afterlife, whether he is a free agent or not, and finally whether life has any meaning or he must give it one (*SU* 145). It is the same yearning for unity that motivates him to devise a "system" in philosophy, to impose a "pattern" on life and to cultivate "form" in art. With the implicit belief in life's disorder at the back of his mind, he defines "a plot" as "merely the pattern on which the story is arranged" (*SU* 130). Hence he would have the author fix upon "his material a willful shape" (*SU* 124) and the novelist draw "a pattern" (*Vagrant Mood* 204). Maugham's devotion to "system", "pattern" and "form" both presupposes and promotes his intellectual consistency, his artistic integrity.

Maugham's lifelong quest is for an all-inclusive unifying vision, which subsumes his pursuit of "system", "pattern" and "form". Since his deliverance on this vital issue figures in somebody else's memoirs, it needs to be quoted at length:

> Rhythm, I suppose, is the...major element in the organization of the universe.... Consider that almost every object is rhythmic in the sense that it is a repetition of a...pattern.... From this, it's only a short... bridge to form. One might say that a non-rhythmic thing is lacking in form. All the words surrounding this idea...mean the same thing in the end, don't they? Rhythm. Form. Tempo. Pace. Organization. Balance. Form. That, I suppose has been the major preoccupation of my life. Form. (Quoted in Garson Kanin 14)

This is as close as Maugham ever comes to directly enunciating the essentially dialectical framework within which he studies everything from the cosmos to man. In his vision of the primordial cosmic rhythm, "the two forces of cosmical attraction and repulsion balanced so that the universe remained for untold ages in a state of perfect equilibrium" (*SU* 157). Man as a microcosm, Maugham seems to think, epitomizes the macrocosm. In any case, strong opposites cohere in his image of man: "Selfishness and kindliness, idealism and sensuality, vanity, shyness, disinterestedness, courage, laziness, nervousness, obstinacy, and diffidence, they can all exist in a single person and form a plausible harmony" (*SU* 41). Maugham "has labored with the utmost sincerity", insists Aldington, "to discover what he really does think and feel, what sort of things he really wishes to do" (*Somerset Maugham* 12). Maugham himself, however, disclaims any originality for his philosophical ideas (*SU* 152). His affinity with Schopenhauer on the point under discussion is striking. Thus Schopenhauer on rhythm, to begin with: "*Rhythm* is in time what *symmetry* is in space, namely the division into equal parts corresponding to one another, and first into larger parts that are again divisible into smaller parts subordinate to the former" (*The World as Will* 2: 453). As Maugham's, so Schopenhauer's definition of rhythm may do duty for that of dialectic, antinomy or polarity. Maugham's universal principle is not substantially different from Schopenhauer's "*polarity*". It is the "sundering of a force into two qualitatively different and opposite activities striving for reunion". What is more, it "is a fundamental type of almost all the phenomena of nature, from the magnet and the crystal up to man" (*WWR* I: 143-44). What both Maugham and Schopenhauer are suggesting here is that since the same absolute manifests itself through everything, the same principle works everywhere. This belief in the oneness of the entire universe and of all life forms is the central tenet of both absolute idealism and of mysticism.

At the present state of Maugham scholarship, it is almost impossible to sidestep the subject of his homosexuality and its repercussions on his art. Soon after his death, Robin Maugham made public as far back as 1966 Maugham's homosexuality. He claims to reproduce Maugham's very words that "I tried to persuade myself that I was three-quarters normal and that only a quarter of me was queer—whereas really it was the other way round" (201). So Maugham's homosexuality is by now old hat: it has lost whatever shock value it once had. Nevertheless it continues to bulk so large especially in his recent biographies that it almost sidetracks his art. The irony is that the critics themselves fail to trace the impact of Maugham's sexual deviation upon his art. Thus Morgan concedes that Maugham "avoided dealing with homosexuality in his work, with two exceptions". He then further adds that "there was in his fiction no major (or minor) homosexual character" (39). "Reading Maugham's fiction", confesses Ivor Brown, "gives no impression that the author was in fact abnormal" (76). Calder's considered view is that "A complete re-reading and revision of Maugham will not therefore uncover a canon of homosexual works" (*Willie* 237). The theoretically-grounded Holden's denial is more emphatic: "Homosexuality does not provide overt thematic content for any of Maugham's fiction" (8). Logic demands that "if Maugham's homosexuality had damaged his reputation" (Hastings 497), its excessive detailing should have been avoided.

Paradoxical though it may sound, Maugham's homosexuality is not altogether detrimental to his art; quite the contrary. Crediting Maugham with the creation of vibrant women characters and the nuanced exploration of their erotic emotions, Marlow thinks he is like "a gynecologist who has the rare ability to, as it were, 'become' his patients" (163). Hastings attributes Maugham's exceptional empathy with women to "his own divided sexuality", which gives "him a kind of double vision, a deeper insight into the feminine psyche" (78). Robin Maugham sees an analogue of the conflict between Maugham's intellect and his instinct in the struggle between his sexual repression and his artistic expression at the heart of his personal and creative life: "I believe that if he hadn't been tortured by desires which in his heart he despised, he wouldn't have written as he did, and he wouldn't have written as excitedly" (Quoted in Meyers 106). Capping all is Maugham's glowing tribute to the memory of Gerald Haxton, the secret love of his life, the alleged wrecker of his marriage, the acknowledged facilitator of his art:

> Without him I should never have written those stories which did so much for my reputation in the world of letters & it was he who helped me to get out of the commonplace life of the ordinary humdrum writer & put me in the way of gaining that wider experience of life which has made me what I am today. (Maugham's letter to Ellen Doubleday quoted in Hastings 476)

Notwithstanding all that has been said above, the real impact of Maugham's homosexuality would continue to elude unless it is studied within the overall framework of his theory of art and originality, of evil and mysticism.

For all his pessimism, Schopenhauer strikes a positive note when he states that "everywhere in nature a remedy, or at any rate a compensation, is given for every evil" (*WWR* II: 463). As a believer in the ultimate unity or oneness of things, Maugham too assigns evil a mitigating role in the realm of art. "It is not always the most worthy men", observes Maugham at his provocative best, "who write the best books" (*Books and You* 41). He singles out Emerson to support his remark: "Perhaps he would have been a better writer if he had not been quite so good a man" (*Books and You* 90). Notorious for his "moral character", Poe is Maugham's counterexample. "Poe wrote", in Maugham's view, "the most beautiful poetry that has ever been written in America" (*Books and You* 91-92). The deeper implication of Maugham's contention is the radical discontinuity between the man and the creator in an artist, between his life and his art. That he reiterates the same idea elsewhere leaves no doubt that it is not his passing whim but his firm conviction: "For unfortunately talent and originality do not always attend nobility of character" (*Selected Prefaces* 29). He presents Dostoevsky as the prime exemplar of his thesis: "It was not the good in Dostoevsky, it was the bad that was the source of the startling originality which made him one of the supreme novelists of the world" (*Ten Novels* 278).

Maugham's unargued assertion about the causal relation between the immorality and originality of the artist may be explained thus. Good thrives on self-effacement which encourages passivity, evil on self-assertion which demands activity. Good puts a premium on simplicity, evil on ingenuity. There is only one way of being good. The resultant sameness invests it with it an air of insipidity. Conversely there are as many ways of being evil as there are evil-doers. Another name for the exciting diversity associated with evil is originality or novelty. Rugged individualists as they are, both the immoralist and the artist live and operate beyond the pale of coercive social morality, which fosters conformity. The foregoing is just a lead-up to the clincher that follows. What clinches Maugham's thesis are the real-life examples he piles up. As in his image of man, so in his portrait of the artist, Maugham juxtaposes strong contraries. Thus "Beethoven's idealism" coexists with "his meanness of spirit", "Wagner's heavenly rapture with his selfishness and dishonesty", "Cervantes' moral obliquity with his tenderness and magnanimity" (*SU* 135). Obviously, as the constituents of an individual with interdependent parts and whole, the coexisting good and evil complement rather than exclude each other. Maugham begins with the proposition that "the composer of the quintent in the Meistersinger was dishonest in money matters and treacherous to those who had benefited him". From this he argues to the conclusion that "it may be that he could not have had great qualities if he had not also had great failings" (*SU* 42). The monist Maugham has to accommodate in his scheme of things good and evil, as all other opposites, as the integral parts of a single whole. Interestingly Russell too generalizes that "It is difficult to think of any instance of a poet who was 'good' at the times when he was writing good poetry" (*Sceptical Essays* 78).

It is now time to come straight to Maugham's theory about the artists' sexual deviation as a factor in their creative originality. Instead of expounding it directly, Maugham manages to insinuate it into his studies of three as diverse subjects as the painter El Greco and the novelists Herman Melville and Emily Bronte. He, however, generalizes a trifle tangentially that "those who possess an aesthetic sense of unusual delicacy diverge sexually from the norm to an extreme and often pathological degree" (*SU* 176-77). Now to return to Maugham's case studies beginning with El Greco. "In the case of El Greco", Morgan somewhat misleadingly comments, "he is writing from the viewpoint of a heterosexual author who belittles homosexuality" (40). Maugham does not openly denounce homosexuality even though he always writes on it from the point of view of a heterosexual. This is because "in the depth of every homosexual there is an anti-homosexual" (Proust, *By Way of Saint-Beuve* 163). For this reason, Maugham conflates homosexuality with immorality, and feels guilty for his own sexual aberration. Interestingly in none of Maugham's three cases is there any incontrovertible evidence of homosexuality, however persuasive his own arguments. Hence there is a lurking suspicion that he uses his subjects as a peg to hang on them his ingenious thesis. In the case of El Greco, Maugham begins by citing Pacheco's testimony that "he was a great philosopher, very witty in his speech, personal, profound, with an original answer to everything" (*Don Fernando* 115). Struck by the painter's singularity, he wonders "whether what I see in El Greco's work of tortured fantasy and sinister strangeness is not due to such a sexual abnormality as this" (*Don Fernando* 116). Finally he rounds off his portrait of El Greco by projecting him, not as convention does, as a religious but as a secular mystic:

> If mysticism is that state that renders you conscious of depths of truth unknown to the intellect, revealing like "glimpses of forgotten dreams" a greater significance in life and union with some larger reality, then I think you can hardly fail to find it in El Greco's painting. (*Don Fernando* 124)

In El Greco Maugham thus aligns homosexuality with originality and mysticism. Nietzsche would certainly bless his enterprise. For he firmly believes that "The degree and nature of a man's sexuality extends to the highest altitudes of his spirit" (*Beyond Good and Evil* 453).

Maugham brings together for the first time in *Books and You* (1940) three such diverse novelists as the American Melville, the British Emily Bronte and the Russian Dostoevsky on the grounds of their shared uniqueness: "There is nothing in fiction that remotely resembles the novels of Dostoevsky except the *Wuthering Heights* of our Emily Bronte and Melville's *Moby Dick*, and *The Brothers Karamazov* is the most tremendous of all Dostoevsky's works" (*Books and You* 58). This is actually a dry run for Maugham's more mature thesis enunciated fourteen years later in *Ten Novels and Their Authors*. Maugham envisages in this book the mainstream European novel, originating with the Greek Longus and flowing up to the French Falubert, as something of a monolith with only minor variations along the way. Its direct purpose has been to amuse by a succession of scenes presented from nature, and by a thread of emotional narrative. Both in terms of their intention and of their effect on the reader, "*Moby Dick*, *Wuthering Heights* and *The Brothers Karamazov*" and "the novels of Joyce and Kafka" (*Ten Novels* 198) constitute a distinct group of their own with originality, intensity and power as their hallmark.

Maugham is struck by Melville's "transformation" from an "apparently normal young man into the savage", pessimistic author of*Pierre*, from the "undistinguished writer of *Typee* into the darkly, imaginative, powerful, inspired and eloquent author of *Moby Dick*". He conceives Melville as "a repressed homosexual", and concludes that "a sexual frustration occasioned the change in him" (*Ten Novels* 210, 214). In a nutshell, Maugham's thesis is that Melville's repressed, frustrated homosexual instinct releases his explosive creative instinct but only for a brief spell. It then extinguishes altogether his creative spark rather prematurely. Maugham's ultimate image of Melville, formed on re-reading *Moby Dick*, is that of "a man endowed by nature with a great gift blighted by an evil genius" (*Ten Novels* 225). Significantly Melville's vision of life, as Maugham extracts it from *Moby Dick*, is pronouncedly metaphysical-mystical: "There is a throb, a mystery, a foreboding, a passion, a sense of the horror and terror of life, of the inevitableness of destiny and of the power of evil, which take you by the throat. You are left shattered, but strangely uplifted" (*Books and You* 98). Maugham unhesitatingly hails *Moby Dick* as a great book and Melville as El Greco's spiritual double.

Maugham first portrays Emily Bronte as a hermaphrodite. He then suggests that she embodies her masculine self in Heathcliff, her feminine in Catherine. Excessively shy and secretive, and so forced to repress it, Emily Bronte has to seek in her art alone an outlet for her fierce emotion. Maugham says the same of Charlotte Bronte. "The two sisters", Maugham holds, "constructed them [Rochester and Heathcliff] to satisfy their urgent, thwarted desires for sexual satisfaction" (*Ten Novels* 256). The nineteen-year-old Emily writes her love poems while teaching at a girls' school at Law Hill. From her emotionally charged love poems, Maugham infers that "they pointed very clearly to her having fallen in love, to her love having been repulsed, and then to her having been bitterly hurt". Since her encounter with a man there is almost improbable, "it is likely enough that she fell in love with one or other of the mistresses, or with one of the girls. It was the only love of her life" (*Ten Novels* 257-58). It is the fire of Emily's frustrated lesbian love that ignites the creation of *Wuthering Heights*. A mark of the novel's "astonishing originality" is that it does not reflect its age either in its technique, in its theme or in its moral vision. Its extraordinariness as a love novel lies in that "the lovers remain chaste" (*Ten Novels* 247, 254). It is Emily Bronte's mysticism that interests Maugham greatly. A genuine mystic, she has written a number of mystical poems. What is more, her mysticism derives not from her reading but from her personal experience. In her famous mystical poem "The Prisoner", she uses, Maugham claims, "almost the very words that the mystics use when they describe the anguish felt of the return from union with the Infinite" (*Ten Novels* 257).

In the case of El Greco, Melville and Emily Bronte, it is their alleged homosexuality that accounts for their originality. The heterosexual Dostoevsky has instead a number of glaring failings such as excessive conceit, jealousy, suspiciousness, masochism and complete lack of willpower, his equivalent of homosexuality. Anyway Maugham's observation about Dostoevsky applies to them as well: "It was not the good in Dostoevsky, it was the bad that was the source of the startling originality which made him one of the supreme novelists of the world" (*Ten Novels* 278). Expectedly Maugham admires Dostoevsky's metaphysical-mystical life vision. He remarks of*The Brothers Karamazov* that "It has a theme of profound significance. Many critics have said that this was the quest of God; I, for my part, should have said it was the problem of evil" (*Ten Novels* 288). El Greco is Maugham's touchstone of mysticism. Maugham likens the incomparable *Wuthering Heights* "only to one of those great pictures of El Greco" (*Ten Novels* 258). The similarity between El Greco and Dostoevsky, however, runs much deeper. Extremely emotional, violently passionate, both wrestle with the problem of making the invisible visible:

> Both give the effect of having walked in unknown ways of the spirit in countries where men do not breathe the air of common day. Both

> are tortured by the desire to express some tremendous secret, which they divine with some sense other than our five senses and which they struggle in vain to convey by use of them. (*WN* 131)

The thesis that an artist's immorality or homosexuality gives a fillip to his originality and induces him to mysticism that Maugham assiduously develops over the decades must have a personal application.

The fact that the homosexual Maugham is a mystic has practically been ignored, a fact that has the potential for revolutionizing Maugham studies and rehabilitating him. He has been a frequent subject of what is technically called ecstasy. It is an educated guess that he was vouchsafed, during his first ever visit to Egypt in January-March of 1906, the ecstasy he very sensitively renders in *The Summing Up*:

> Indeed, I have myself had on one occasion an experience that I could only describe in the words the mystics have used to describe their ecstasy. I was sitting in one of the deserted mosques near Cairo when suddenly I felt myself rapt as Ignatius of Loyola was rapt when he sat by the river at Manresa. I had an overwhelming sense of the power and import of the universe, and an intimate, a shattering sense of communion with it. I could almost bring myself to say that I felt the presence of God. (*SU* 160)

Similarly he had, during his India tour in 1938, another experience of ecstasy, which was triggered by the very sight of the famed Taj Mahal:

> […] I was overcome by its beauty. I recognized that this was the authentic thrill of art and tried to examine myself while it was still vivid. I can understand that when people say something takes their breath away it is not an idle metaphor. I really did feel shortness of breath. I had a queer, delightful feeling in my heart, as though it were dilated. I felt surprise and joy and, I think, a sense of liberation:…. (*WN* 230)

His delicate sensitivity to beauty occasions his ecstasy so often that he would seem to have been a habitual ecstatic: "Indeed on occasion, looking at certain pictures or statues, listening to certain music, I have had an emotion so strong that I could only describe it in the same words as those the mystics use to describe the union with God." What with his secular triggers for and his secular mode of attaining ecstasy, Maugham feels justified in thoroughly secularizing mysticism. What is more, he stubbornly refuses to subordinate secular mysticism to religious: "That is why I have thought that this sense of communion with a larger reality is not only the privilege of the religious, but may be reached by other paths than prayer and fasting" (*SU* 177-78). It is as well that Maugham universalizes mysticism by conceiving everybody as a potential mystic: "If the mystical experience is a liberating sense of community with what for want of a better word we name reality, and this you can call as you will the Absolute or God, then at some time we are all in greater or less degree mystics" (*Don Fernando* 125).

Spurred on by his own mystical experience, Maugham reads widely in the mystical literature of the world just a fragment of which he shares with the reader. He has in his collection the complete fifteen-volume set of Baring-Gould's *Lives of the Saints*. On occasion he dips into them to satisfy his curiosity of the moment. In addition, "I have read the autobiography of St. Theresa and the lives, written by those who knew them, of St. Francis of Assisi, of Catherine of Siena, and of Ignatius of Loyola" (*Points of View* 56). No less keen is his interest in Eastern mysticism. Despite his avowed modesty, his knowledge of the subject, for a lay Westerner, is almost thorough:

> What I know about it, I have read in books. The most important of these are Sir Charles Elliot's *Hinduism and Buddhism*; Radhakrishnan's *History of Indian Philosophy* and his translation of the Upanishads; Krishnaswami Iyer's *Vedanta*, or the *Science of Reality*; *Brahma-Knowledge* by Professor Barnett; and Sankara's *Vivekachudamani*. (*Points of View* 61)

It needs to be stressed that his interest in Vedantism is more than academic. He felt at one time so drawn to it that he yo-yoed with the idea of making it his personal philosophy: "Faced with it, [the ultimate mystery], awed by the greatness of the universe and malcontent what the philosophers told me, and what with the saints, I have sometimes gone back, beyond Mohammed, Jesus and Buddha, beyond the gods of Greece, Jehovah and Baal, to the Brahma of Upanisads" (*SU* 160). A measure of his absorption into Vedantism is his unrealized plan to visit India for a second time in order to write a life of Sankara who fascinated him. On top of this, the catalogue of Maugham's personal library, gifted to his alma mater, King's School, Canterbury, details a large number of other titles on Eastern and Western mysticism. More importantly, it informs that Maugham annotated William James's *Varieties of Religious Experience* and Bertrand Russell's *Mysticism and Logic*. In view of all this Meyers's *ipse dixit* that Maugham "didn't have a mystical bone in his body" (230) seems quite astounding.

Maugham's first mystical experience, ecstasy, dates tentatively from 1906; his success as a popular dramatist from 1907. So his mysticism and his freedom, economic and spiritual, come hard on the heels of each other. His new vision urges him to strike out on his own; his new economic freedom adds momentum to that yearning for novelty. No wonder, while working on *Of Human Bondage*, his first mystical masterpiece, he is seized by the idea (in August 1911) that originality is the novel's only *raison d'être*: "So many novels are written in these days that there seems no reason to write one unless it is out of the common, except the pleasure it gives the writer; & that, thank heaven, is something that is independent of the result" (Maugham's letter cited in Hastings 159). It is no coincidence that, on the novel's completion, he asserts his total artistic integrity in contrast to many of his compeers' penchant for compromise: "Many writers are forced by poverty to consider whether this or that will hurt the sale of their books [...] but I think it would be disgraceful if I allowed any such thoughts to influence me" (Maugham letter cited in Hastings 166). Maugham's simmering discontent, as manifest in the two quotes above, further fuelled by his discovery in 1917 of the radically different Russian novel, reaches a boiling point. He assails the whole of the West European novel for its emotional and intellectual monotony, most of all for its crass philistinism: "It was a fiction fit for a middle-class civilization, well-fed, well-clothed, well-housed, and its readers were resolute to bear in mind that all they read was make-believe" (*WN* 113-14). Not content with savaging an entire novel tradition, he now singles out three of the West's top-drawer novelists whose native gifts he admires but whose values he abominates. "Of all the great novelists", Maugham claims, "that have enriched with their works the spiritual treasures of the world, Balzac is to my mind the greatest". He thus builds Balzac up only to demolish him: "He had achieved his aim: I don't suppose it ever occurred to Balzac that it was a vulgar one" (*Ten Novels* 109, 136-37). Dickens too fails to measure up to Maugham's rigorous standard of "high seriousness". "For all their great merits", Maugham thinks that "Dickens's [novels] are scarcely adult" (*Ten Novels* 159). Maugham's response to Henry James follows the set pattern. He appreciates James's "humour, insight, subtlety, a sense of drama". He, however, deplores his "triviality of soul that made the elemental emotions of mankind, love and hatred, the fear of death and the sense of life's mystery, incomprehensible to him" (*Books and You* 93-94). The fact that Maugham's invariable targets are values and visions points to his mysticism as the source of his iconoclasm. There is a positive side to Maugham's denunciation of the fictional giants inasmuch as it serves to define him by implication. It would seem that Maugham himself is free from Balzac's vulgarity and Dickens's intellectual immaturity. And the exploration of mankind's elemental emotions is his forte.

What Maugham's homosexuality and his mysticism bring to the fore is the relation between the man and the writer in him, the relation between his life and his art. He claims to "have put the whole of my life into my books" (*SU* 6) and to have carried out "in my own life certain actions which I made the characters of my invention do" (*SU* 30). His art feeds on his life in other ways too. It is the writer's lived experience, the experience that bears the impress of his body and mind, ultimately of his whole personality, and especially his felt life that serve as the raw material. That is why verbal art is, Maugham argues, necessarily autobiographical: "Most of what one writes is to a greater or lesser degree autobiographical, not the actual incidents always, but always the emotions" (Maugham's letter to Violet Hunt, excerpted in Hastings 93). In the case of a novelist, the autobiographical basis of his art extends further. Maugham reasons that a novelist succeeds in creating living characters only when he fleshes out his own potential selves. It follows then that by studying the novelist's most successful and sympathetic characters, "you should be able to get a more complete idea of his nature than any biography can give you" (*WN* 279). Maugham pushes this argument to its logical extreme, invokes the romantic or expressive theory of art, and pictures the novelist as a compulsive, albeit oblique, autobiographer: "Whatever he [the novelist] writes is the expression of his personality and it is the manifestation of his innate instincts, his feelings and his experiences" (*Ten Novels* 8-9). This inevitably leads to Maugham's theory of art as purgation. A writer can use his painful experience as material for his art, and by "writing it he can overcome it" (*SU* 111). This intimacy between life and art justifies Maugham's prescription that "to know what sort of a person the author was adds to one's understanding and appreciation of his work" (*Ten Novels* 20). Identity between the man and the writer is, however, one term of Maugham's dialectic; dichotomy between them is the other.

An artist's art invariably preys on his life. His creative instinct is an inexorable force which makes him dead to everything else outside his art, and so turns him into a virtual monomaniac. Accordingly Maugham generalizes that the artists "succumb to an influence they do not realize and life slips through their fingers unlived" (Preface, *Collected Plays* I: xviii). So ruthless is Maugham's own artistic devotion that he allows nothing to stand between him and his work. Naturally he places the artist's work above his happiness. The act of creation is so absorbing, so exhilarating that any idea of returning to the human activities of everyday life strikes an artist as a terrible comedown, and so fills him with dismay. Speaking for himself as for his compeers, Maugham says: "Most authors, when engaged on a work of fiction, are so absorbed in it that they can think of nothing else, and when they give up for the day exhausted, look upon the rest of it with impatience as so much time lost till next day they can set to work again" (*Points of View* 22). What wonder then that Maugham should have confessed that "I have always enjoyed writing," but "I have never enjoyed living" (cited in Kanin 165).

The self the polypsychic artist enshrines in his art may have its very antagonist lurking within him. That is why however sincere he may be in his creative emotion, "there is someone else within him who is capable of cocking a snook at its exercise" (*SU* 136). The difference between the author's man-self and his artist-self is at its maximum in the case of sublimation. As Maugham explains it: "Every creative writer's work is, to some extent at least, a sublimation of instincts, desires, day-dreams …which for one cause or another he had repressed, and by giving them literary expression he is freed of the compulsion to give them the further release of action" (*Ten Novels* 307). Maugham's explanation of the yawning gulf between an author's life and his art has its close parallel in Kierkegaard's. Being a poet means, thinks Kierkegaard, "having one's own personal life, one's reality in quite different categories from those of one's poetic work, it means being related to the ideal in imagination only, so that one's own personal life is more or less a satire on poetry and on oneself" (153). Maugham uses Dostoevsky to dramatize the distance between a writer's life and his art:

> I can think of no one in whom the dichotomy between the man and the writer has been greater than it was in Dostoevsky. It probably exists in all creative artists, but it is more conspicuous in authors than in others because their medium is words, and the contradiction between their behavior and their communication is more shocking. (*Ten Novels* 278)

It is worth noting in this context that Maugham stresses the polarity between life and art in the cases of Melville, Emily Bronte and Dostoevsky whom he groups together as his favourites. By implication, what is true of his spiritual affinities is true of him as well.

The artist's polypsychism brings into sharp focus the question of his real self. Maugham has implicitly answered this question in his portrait of Burke as a divided self: "In his study he was no longer the reckless punter, the shameless sponge, the unscrupulous place-hunter... the dishonest advocate.... In his study he was the high-minded man whom his friends loved and honoured for his nobility of spirit, his greatness and his magnanimity" (*Vagrant Mood* 141). Maugham is more forthright when he claims of Goethe that "[h]e was his true self only when he wrote poetry" (*Points of View* 50). Likewise Proust too asserts that "the writer's true self is manifested in his books alone" (*By Way of Saint-Beuve* 81). Maugham's intense aversion to his biography admits of many explanations. A literary biography is normally premised on the man-writer identity which is unacceptable to Maugham. He lives his real life not within the public world of society but within the private world of his mind. It is not without reason that Pico Iyer challenges the efficacy of Maugham's biographical criticism:

> To use the life to understand the work,..., is to try to explain the larger self by the smaller; to use the work to shed light on the life is to begin to understand how a figure who looked buttoned up and unfeeling at the dinner table could write books that hold readers with their openness and warmth. (72)

As a matter of fact, Maugham himself uses *Moby Dick* as a clue to understanding Melville the man, and thereby recants his cherished recipe for novel-reading:

> I have said, and said again, that in order to get a real insight into a great novel you must know what there is to be known about the man who wrote it. I have an idea that in the case of Melville something like the contrary obtains. When one reads, and re-reads, *Moby Dick*, it seems to me that one gets a more convincing, a more definite, impression of the man than from anything one may learn of his life and circumstances; [...]. (*Ten Novels* 225)

Echoing Maugham, one may say that immersion in his major novels alone would offer a glimpse of his essential self. His homosexuality would then seem his husk, his mysticism his kernel.

At the end of this overview, the question that remains to be answered is whether Maugham has received his just deserts. His own answer may serve as a piquant starter: "In my twenties the critics said I was brutal, in my thirties they said I was flippant, in my forties they said I was cynical, in my fifties they said I was competent, and now in my sixties they say I am superficial" (*SU* 132). The reasons for Maugham's pique are still there. True, he has been receiving, particularly since his death, steadily increasing critical attention. A couple of examples would show how Maugham continues to be misunderstood and underestimated as ever. Beverly Nichols refuses to grant Maugham even a consistent philosophy: "It is a dramatist's philosophy.... There is no basic rhythm to the thought" (105). More devastating is Raphael. He discerns a thinness of "metaphysical and symbolical allusion" in Maugham, and so pronounces that "He was too clear to be great" (99). Maugham is too sophisticated to indulge in literary exhibitionism. He would like the writer to have "a distinguished and varied culture", but not to put "its elements into his work" (*WN* 217). Another critic snipes at both Maugham and Maugham scholarship, and demands that Maugham's seriousness "is something that should be shown, not asserted" ("Just Visiting" 67). Calder acutely diagnoses the shortcomings of current Maugham studies, and prescribes the remedies: "At this stage of Maugham criticism...the need is not for another general survey, but more specialized examinations of particular patterns, techniques, devices, and ideas" (Rev. of*The Pattern of Maugham* 189). Contrary to Calder's prescription, it is not the critics but the biographers of Maugham who have been in recent years ruling the roost.

The irony is that Maugham himself laments his contemporaries' lack of seriousness: "Nobody dares tackle great subjects and the heresy has become orthodox that subject is of no consequence" (*Don Fernando* 123). It is for its "extreme triviality" (*SU* 129) that he dismisses the stream-of-consciousness novel as meretricious. As for his own seriousness, he decides to retire as a dramatist, right at the height of his power and popularity, simply because he refuses to tailor his themes to suit the conventions of contemporary theatre: "The fashion of today prevents any reference on the stage to the great subjects of human life and the most profound thoughts of human beings" (*Collected Plays* III: xii). Persistent misunderstanding and underestimate exasperate him so much that he throws for the nonce his wonted modesty to the winds, and flaunts his seriousness:

> Though my literary friends do not, I am sorry to say, look upon me as a member of the intelligentsia, I very much enjoy the conversation of cultured persons and I think (perhaps mistakenly) that I can adequately hold my own with them. Indeed sometimes I gently lead them down the garden path of mysticism and when I talk to them of Denis the Areopagite and Fray Luis de Leon, throwing in Samkaracharia for good measure, I often have them grasping for breath like speckled trout on a river bank. (*Vagrant Mood* 239-40)

Now a couple of examples to show how much depth there is, beneath their surface simplicity, in Maugham's mature novels. With the consummate skill of an accomplished storyteller, he slips in the core idea of mysticism in *Of Human Bondage*, the most autobiographical of his novels: "It was a mystical city in which the imagination faltered like one who steps out of the light into darkness; the soul walked naked to and fro, knowing the unknowable, and conscious strangely of experience, intimate but inexpressible, of the absolute" (670). How demanding a writer Maugham would appear from the following apparently simple sentence from *Cakes and Ale*, which in fact encapsulates the quintessence of absolute idealism and mysticism: "I had an impression that the real man, to his death unknown and lonely, was a wraith that went a silent way unseen between the writer of his books and the man who led his life, and smiled with ironical detachment at the two puppets that the world took for Edward Driffield" (224). Despite his manifest seriousness, Maugham's entrenched critical image as a popular entertainer provokes him ultimately to challenge his critics: "The critic I am waiting for is the one who will explain why, with all my faults, I have been read for so many years by so many people" (Maugham's letter cited in Morgan 586). As he has answered almost all questions about himself, he also responds to his challenge, indirectly though. Trying to pinpoint what contributes most to a novelist's greatness, he concludes that

> The four greatest novelists the world has ever known, Balzac, Dickens, Tolstoy and Dostoevsky, wrote their respective languages very indifferently. It proves that if you can tell stories, create character, devise incidents, and if you have sincerity and passion, it doesn't matter a damn how you write. (*WN* 255)

Maugham's twofold strategy here is to minimize his weakness and to highlight his strength. If the four named novelists can achieve greatness despite their indifferent style, Maugham's plain style, his detractors' invariable target, cannot be a serious handicap. As for the other requisites for greatness that Maugham specifies, he has them in abundance. All in all, Maugham's title to greatness may be debated but not his title to seriousness. He himself is what he exhorts the writer to be: "playful and serious at the same time" (*WN* 209). Unfortunately his playfulness has been appreciated to the near-total exclusion of his seriousness. To be fair to him, the balance needs to be redressed.

WORKS CITED

Aldington, Richard. *Somerset Maugham: An Appreciation.* New York: Doubleday, Doran, 1939.

Brown, Ivor. *W. Somerset Maugham*. London: International Textbook Company, 1970.

Calder, Robert. *Willie: The Life of W. Somerset Maugham*. 1989. Rpt. London: Mandarin, 1990.

——"Rev. of *The Pattern of Maugham*" by Anthony Curtis. *The Critical Quarterly*. 17 (Summer 1975): 188-89.

Ewing, A.C. *The Fundamental Questions of Philosophy*. 1951. Rpt. New Delhi: Allied, 1989.

Ewing, A.C. *Idealism: A Critical Survey*. 1934. Rpt. London: Methuen, 1961.

Hastings, Selina. *The Secret Lives of Somerset Maugham*. 2009. Rpt. London: John Murray, 2010.

Holden, Philip. *Orienting Masculinity, Orienting Nation: W. Somerset Maugham's Exotic Fiction*. London: Greenwood, 1996.

Iyer, Pico. "Summing Him Up". *The New York Review*. December 16, 2004: 72-75.

Jung, C.G. *Modern Man in Search of a Soul*. Trans. W.S. Dell and Cary F. Baynes. 1933. Rpt. London: Routledge, 1962.

Kanin, Garson. *Remembering Mr. Maugham*. London: Hamish Hamilton, 1966.

Kierkegaard, Soren. *The Journals of Kierkegaard*. Trans. Alexander Dree. New York: Harper, 1959.

Laing, R.D. *The Divided Self: An Existentialist Study in Sanity and Madness*. 1960. Rpt. Harmondsworth: Penguin Books, 1981.

Marlow, Louis. *Seven Friends*. London: The Richards Press, 1953.

Maugham, Robin. *Somerset and All the Maughams*. London: Longmans, 1966.

Maugham, W. Somerset. *A Writer's Notebook*. 1949. Rpt. *The Partial View*. London: Heinemann, 1954.

——. *Books and You*. New York: Doubleday, Doran, 1940.

——. *Cakes and Ale: Or the Skeleton in the Cupboard*. 1930. Rpt. London: Heinemann, 1979.

——. *Don Fernando*. 1935. Rpt. *The Travel Books of W. Somerset Maugham*. London: Heinemann, 1955.

——. *Of Human Bondage*. 1915. Rpt. London: Heinemann, 1956.

——. *On a Chinese Screen*. 1922. Rpt. *The Travel Books of W. Somerset Maugham*.

——. *Points of View*. 1958. Rpt. London: Heinemann, 1960.

——. *Selected Prefaces and Introductions of W. Somerset Maugham*. London: Heinemann, 1963.

——. *Ten Novels and their Authors*. 1954. Rpt. London: Vintage, 2001.

——. *The Collected Plays of W. Somerset Maugham*. 1931. Rpt. London: Heinemann, 1961.

——. *The Gentleman in the Parlour*. 1930. Rpt. *The Travel Books of W. Somerset Maugham*.

——. *The Summing Up*. 1933. Rpt. *The Partial View*. London: Heinemann, 1954.

——. *The Vagrant Mood: Six Essays*. London: Heinemann, 1952.

——. *The Writer's Point of View*. Cambridge University Press, 1951.

"Just Visiting". "Rev. of *The Pattern of Maugham*" by Anthony Curtis. *Times Literary Supplement* 25 Jan. 1974: 67.

Meyers, Jeffrey. *Somerset Maugham: A Life*. 2004. Rpt. New York: Vintage, 2005.

Morgan, Ted. *Somerset Maugham*. London: Jonathan Cape, 1980.

Nichols, Beverley. *A Case of Human Bondage*. London: Secker & Warburg, 1966.

Nietzsche, *Beyond Good and Evil*. Trans. H. Zimmern. *The Philosophy of Nietzsche*. Intro. W.H. Wright. 1927. Rpt. New York: Random House, 1954.

Proust, Marcel. *By Way of Saint-Beuve*. Trans. S.T. Warner. London: Chatto & Windus, 1958.

Raphael, Frederic. *W. Somerset Maugham and His World*. London: Thames & Hudson, 1976.

Russell, Bertrand. *Sceptical Essays*. 1935. Rpt. London: Unwin, 1970.

Schopenhauer, Arthur. *The World as Will and Representation*. Trans. E.F.J. Payne. 1958. Rpt. New York: Dover, 1966.

❑❑❑

Walden: A Spiritual Autobiography

BASAVARAJ NAIKAR

WRITING one's autobiography is indeed a very difficult and delicate task. An autobiography presupposes a very rich and intense experience on the part of its author. Since it is an expression of the picture of the relationship between the individual self and the external world, its success and greatness depend more upon the honesty of its expression than upon the linguistic efficiency of expression. Thoreau's *Walden* happens to be a model of such an autobiography, which deals not with the entirety of his life, but confines itself only to that part of his life in which he experimented with the external world to derive maximum spiritual enlightenment and satisfaction. Thus *Walden*, though partial in its coverage of his physical life, is intended to represent his pursuit of spiritual unity and wholeness. It can, therefore, be described as his spiritual autobiography, which easily invites comparison with Mahatma Gandhi's *The Story of My Experiments with Truth.*

Deeply disillusioned with the American materialism and utilitarianism, Thoreau wanted to escape to the woods and find spiritual consolation in the midst of Nature near the Walden Pond between 1845 and 1847. In this autobiography he records his gradual growth from the material plane to the spiritual plane, through innumerable meticulous details. His departure to the woods corresponds to that of a *vanaprastha*, who tries to seek spiritual happiness in the midst of a forest by living in the company of non-human creatures. Thus the stay in the woods naturally helps Thoreau to have the privacy necessary to observe and meditate upon the mystery of life thereby consolidating his spiritual strength and controlling his distracting senses. Thus loneliness, far from being a punishment, happens to be a boon to a spiritual aspirant like Thoreau.

The autobiography shows the stage by stage growth of its author. For example, the first chapter entitled "Economy" shows how he experimented with the ideal of self-reliance, frugality, sincerity and simplicity:

> When I wrote the following pages, or rather the bulk of them, I lived alone, in the woods, a mile from my neighbor, in a house, which I had built myself, on the shore of Walden Pond, in Concord, Massachusetts, and earned my living by the labor of my hands only. I lived there two years and two months. (Thoreau 1964: 3)

Thoreau's stay in the woods helps him cultivate voluntary poverty, which is very essential for the spiritual enrichment. By poverty, Thoreau means the use of bare necessities of physical life. In his opinion the bare necessities of life are closely connected with self-reliance: "By the words, necessary of life, I mean whatever, of all that man obtains by his own exertions, has been from the first, or from long use has become, so important to human life that few, if any, whether from savageness, of poverty, or philosophy, ever attempt to do without it (*Ibidem* 11). Thoreau practices his philosophy of simplicity in the woods near the Walden Pond by diligently experimenting with the bare necessities of life like shelter, clothing and food and achieving a rare kind of spiritual enlightenment. These experiments are recorded meticulously by him in his spiritual autobiography called *Walden*.

Thoreau recognizes the importance of shelter for all living creatures especially for man. "Man wanted a home, a place of warmth, or comfort, first of physical warmth, then the warmth of the affections" (*Ibidem* 25). But he warns that the shelter—be it a home or a palace—should not restrict his sense of spiritual freedom. Thoreau expresses the same in an epigrammatic fashion, "And when the former has got his house, he may not be the richer but the poorer for it, and it be the house that has got him" (*Ibidem* 30). Continuing the same line of argument, he remarks that "we are often imprisoned rather than housed in them" (*Ibidem* 30). Houses should be neither prisons nor graves, but liberators of human spirit.

The greatness of Thoreau lies in his actualization of all his theoretical beliefs. Shelter, according to him, should provide protection from the elemental forces, wild animals and so forth. It should not be a matter of exhibition. It should protect his body so that the soul could be activated. Shelter should, thus, be a means to an end rather than an end in itself. Thoreau did not become great only by preaching his principles, but by actually practising them thereby setting a personal example for others. He builds his own house by taking great pains: "I dug my cellar in the side of a hill sloping to the south where a woodchuck had formerly dug his burrow, down through sumach and blackberry roots, and the lowest stain of vegetation, six feet square by seven deep, to a fine sand where potatoes would not freeze in any winter…. At length, in the beginning of May, with the help of some of my acquaintances…I set up the frame of my house…. I began to occupy my house on the 4th of July, as soon as it was boarded and roofed…" (*Ibidem* 40). Thoreau did not get a house built by laborers, but he built it all by himself, in accordance with his principles of self-reliance and sanctity of labor. The joy of self-reliance is inexplicable indeed! That is the reason why he says, "There is some of the same fitness in man's building his own house that there is in a bird's building its own nest" (*Ibidem* 41).

Thoreau offers an actual chart of expenses incurred for the building materials like boards, laths, bricks, lime, hair, nails, hinges, screws, latch, chalk and shows the total amount running to only $28.12-1/2. He has thus demonstrated how one can derive maximum comfort in one's shelter with the minimum expenditure. The luxury of architecture could be easily avoided. The architectural ornamentation is something that is empty or redundant: "A great proportion of architectural ornaments are literally hollow, and a September gale would strip them off, like borrowed plumes, without injury to substantials. They can do without architecture, who have no olives nor wines in the cellar" (*Ibidem* 42). Thoreau rightly believes that a house or shelter is an extension of one's personality and a symbol of one's simplicity and detachment.

Thoreau believes in the wearing of simple and minimum clothes and disapproves of luxurious or ornamental clothing. He says, "…the object of clothing is, first, to retain the vital heat, and secondly, in this state of society, to cover nakedness, and he may judge how much of any necessary or important work may be accomplished without adding to his wardrobe" (*Ibidem* 19). He believes that our garments become part of our personalities. "Every day our garments become more and more assimilated to ourselves, receiving the impress of the wearer's character" (*Ibidem* 19).

He believes that food is required for the sustenance of the physical life. If one takes too much of food, it might fatten the body at the cost of spiritual life. True to his convictions, Thoreau experiments with living on the simplest and minimum food: "It appears from the above estimate, that my food alone cost me in money about twenty-seven cents a week. It was, for nearly two years after this, rye and Indian meal without yeast, potatoes, rice, a very little salt port, molasses, and salt, and my drink, water. It was fit that I live on rice mainly, who loved so well the philosophy of India" (*Ibidem* 55). He pleads not only for the simplicity of food, but also for the exercise of the principle of self-reliance in the preparation of one's food. He not only teaches these principles but actually practices them in the woods of Walden: "Bread at first made of pure Indian meal and salt, genuine hoe-cakes, which I baked before my fire out of doors on a shingle or the end of a stick of timber sawed off in building my house; but it was won't to get smoked and to have piney flavor. I tried flour also; but have at last found a mixture of rye and Indian meal most convenient and agreeable" (*Ibidem* 55).

The kind of food recommended by Thoreau is noteworthy. He insists on vegetarian food: "There is a certain class of unbelievers, who sometimes ask me such questions as if I think that I can live on vegetable food alone; and...I am accustomed to answer such that I can live on board nails" (*Ibidem* 58). He strongly recommends the non-vegetarian food on the ground that it is unclean as well as being a hindrance to spiritual purification: "The practical objection to animal food in my case was its uncleanness; and besides, when I had caught and cleaned and cooked and eaten my fish, they seemed not to have fed me essentially. It was insignificant and unnecessary, and cost me more than it came to.... I believe that every man, who has ever been earnest to preserve his higher or poetic faculties in the best condition has been particularly inclined to abstain from animal food, and from much food of any kind" (*Ibidem* 193).

Thoreau's reduction of the necessities of life like food, shelter, clothing and fuel was in line with his concept of simple living and high thinking. "Simplicity, simplicity, simplicity" (*Ibidem* 82) happens to be the chief motto of his life. The principle of simplicity is closely linked with that of voluntary poverty: Thoreau believes that the four necessities of life are required for the maintenance of 'animal life', which is another name for 'animal heat'. He explains it clearly as: "...for while Food may be regarded as the Fuel which keeps up the fire within us—and Fuel serves only to prepare that Food or to increase the warmth of our bodies by addition from without—Shelter and Clothing also serve only to retain the heat thus generated and absorbed" (*Ibidem* 12). Thoreau's belief in the possession of the bare necessities of life and the practice of voluntary poverty are inspired by the view that "Most of the luxuries, and many of the so-called comforts of life, are not only indispensable, but positive hindrances to the elevation of mankind" (*Ibidem* 13). His views are easily comparable to those expressed in the Bible and other scriptures of the world.

Thoreau believes that food is required for the sustenance of physical life. If one takes too much of food, it might fatten the body at the cost of spiritual life. True to his convictions, he experiments with living on the simplest and minimum food: "It appears from the above estimate, that my food alone cost me in money about twenty-seven cents a week. It was, for nearly two years after this, rye and Indian meal without yeast, potatoes, rice, a very little salt port, molasses, and salt; and my drink, water. It was fit that I live on rice mainly, who loved so well the philosophy of India" (*Ibidem* 55). Thoreau pleads not only for the simplicity of food, but also for the exercise of the principle of self-reliance in the preparation of one's food. He not only teaches these principles but actually practices them in the woods of Walden: "Bread I at first made of pure Indian meal and salt, genuine hoe-cakes, which I baked before my fire out of doors on a shingle or the end of a stick of timber sawed off in building my house; but it was wont to get smoked and to have piney flavor. I tried flour also; but have at last found a mixture of rye and Indian meal most convenient and agreeable" (*Ibidem* 55).

The kind of food recommended by Thoreau is noteworthy. He insists on vegetarian food: "There is a certain class of unbelievers, who sometimes ask me such questions as if I think that I can live on vegetable food on board nails" (*Ibdem* 58). He strongly opposes the non-vegetarian food on the ground that it is unclean as well as being a hindrance to spiritual purification: The practical objection to animal food in my case was its uncleanness; and besides, when I had caught and cleansed and cooked and eaten my fish, they seemed not to have fed me essentially. It was insignificant and unnecessary, and cost me more than it came to.... I believe that every man who has ever been earnest to preserve his higher or poetic faculties in the best condition has been particularly inclined to abstain from animal food, and from much food of any kind" (*Ibidem* 193).

Thoreau's reduction of the necessities of life like food, shelter, clothing and fuel was in line with his concept of simple living and high thinking. "Simplicity, simplicity, simplicity" (*Ibidem* 82) happens to be the chief motto of his life. The principle of simplicity is closely linked with that of voluntary poverty: "Most of the luxuries, and many of the so-called comforts of life, are not only indispensable, but positive hindrances to the elevation of mankind. With respect to luxuries and comforts, the wisest have ever lived a more simple and meager life than the poor. The ancient philosophers, Chinese, Hindu, Persian and the Greek were a class than which none has been poorer in outward riches, none so rich in inward.... None can be an impartial or wise observer of human life but from the vantage ground of what we should call voluntary poverty" (*Ibidem* 13).

Thoreau's purpose of going to the woods was to experiment with a life of abstinence and voluntary poverty for the achievement of spiritual enlightenment: "I went to the woods because I wished to live deliberately, to front only the essential facts of life, and see if I could not learn what it had to teach, and not, when I came to die, discover that I had not lived. I did not wish to live what was not life, living is so dear; nor did I wish to practice resignation, unless it was quite necessary. I wanted to live deep and suck all the marrow of life, to live so sturdily and Spartan-like as to put the rout all that was not life, to cut a broad swath and shave close, to drive life into a corner, and reduce it to its lowest terms, and if proved to be mean, why then to get the whole and genuine meanness of it, and publish its meanness to the world; or if it were sublime, to know it by experience, and be able to give a true account of it in my next excursion" (*Ibidem* 82). Thoreau's willingness to participate in the actual experience of living and thereby eke out the deepest joy as well as knowledge of life is evident in his words. His aim was to have the first-hand knowledge of the sublimity of life before writing about it.

Thoreau's minimization of human needs to the bare necessities, his adoption of the principle of simplicity and the practice of the principle of self-reliance expressed mainly through physical labor and his lonely stay in the forest of the Walden Pond were all teleologically directed towards the enlargement of his spiritual personality. All these details of his rigorous discipline were geared to the awakening of higher, i.e. spiritual faculties. His intention happened to be a saintly one in that he wanted to tame the animal in himself thereby awakening the latest angel in him. Thus the whole experimentation was spiritually oriented. As Richard J. Schneider rightly says, "A closer reading of Walden reveals a Thoreau who is often less interested in stasis than in change, less interested in meditation than in a journey of exploration" (Schneider 93). This is not a mere external journey but an "inward exploration" (Sherman Paul 93). As William Drake says, "*Walden*, like the *Week*, has for its structure an elaborated metaphor. It is that of a traveler who, instead of leaving home, explores the very ground he lives on. Only now the end of exploration is in sight and the book points to them from the beginning" (William Drake 71). Thoreau's spirituality was not escapist or life negating, but on the contrary, it happened to be participatory and life affirming. His intention was not to run away from the material, i.e. natural life to search for spiritual life, but to find the latter while in the midst of the former. The details for such a search for the transcendental truths of life could be discussed at some length here.

The first thing that strikes the attention of Thoreau in the woods is, obviously, Nature. Although his stay in the forest is motivated by spiritual goals, the poetic sensibility and the capacity for scientific or microscopic observation are not suppressed or ignored by him. His derivation of spiritual enlightenment is normally preceded by the almost scientific observation of the minute details of the flora and fauna, hills and dales, rivers and land and a poetic appreciation of their beauty. Thoreau's spirituality, far from being a high and dry pursuit, is enlivened by the aesthetic element, which is further supported by the scientific abundance of facts and details. Thus Thoreau, in Kantian terms, endeavors to reach the Noumena through the enjoyment of phenomena. For him, as also for Wordsworth, Nature with all its variegated beauty could be symbolic of higher truths of life. For example, his worship of Nature is an evidence of his high philosophy: "Every morning was a cheerful invitation to make my life of equal simplicity, and I may say innocence, with Nature herself. I have been as sincere a worshipper of Aurora as the Greeks. I got up early and bathed in the pond; that was a religious exercise, and one of the best things which I did" (*Ibidem* 80). As R.W. Desai rightly says, "Thoreau's Walden Pond is one of the best illustrations of Yeats's statement that 'there may be a landscape that is symbolical of some spiritual condition'" (*Autobiographies*, London, 1955: 74).

His stay in the woods enables him to hear a variety of sounds produced by the multitude of things, beings and events of Nature. He hears the whistle of the locomotive and morning cars, the hooting of owls, the barking of dogs, the crowing of cocks and cockerels, the scream of bluejays and the laughing of loons, etc., with real gusto and rapt attention. Through these sounds he seems to hear the divine voice or melody thereby growing ecstatic like a mystic. Many times he compares these sounds with other things or beings and gives expression to his poetic sensibility: "When other birds are still, the screech owls take up the strain, like mourning women their ancient *ululu*. Their dismal scream is truly Ben Jonsonian.... Yet I love to hear their wailing, their doleful responses, trilled along the wood side; reminding me sometime of music and singing birds; as if it were the dark and tearful side of music, the regrets and sighs that would fain be sung. They are the spirits, the low spirits and melancholy foreboding, of fallen souls that once in human shape night-walked the earth and did the deeds of darkness, now expiating their sins with their wailing hymns of threnodies in the scenery of their transgressions. They gave me a new sense of the variety and capacity of that nature, which is our common dwelling" (*Ibidem* 113).

Just as Thoreau was inspired by the variety of sounds of Nature, he was also inspired by the various sights of Nature through which he could drink in the beauty like a poet. As usual, Thoreau combines the scientific method of observation with the philosophical meditation and the poetic expression. The basic method of observation and the indefatigable record of multiple details of natural objects employed by him happen to be scientific and almost photographic. But the process does not end there. Thoreau's mind will be simultaneously meditating about these details until it manifests itself in the form of a generalization. Likewise, his heart will be busy responding to the external world until it experiences a surplus of emotion, which is crystallized in the form of a figure of speech. For example, he observes a numberless things and beings of Nature like pitch pines, birches, alders, aspens, pickerel, water-bugs, mice, cats, robins, partridge, otters, loons, turtle doves with a child-like curiosity and delights in the experience. His eyes notice not only the big and conspicuous things of Nature, but also microscopically observe even the tiniest creatures like ants. His description of the war of ants is a superb example of his microscopic observation: "I was witness to events of a less peaceful character. One day when I went out to my wood-pile, or rather my pile of stumps, I observed two large ants, the one red, the other much larger, nearly half an inch long, and black, fiercely contending with one another. Having once got hold they never let go, but struggled and wrestled and rolled on the chips incessantly.... It was the only battle, which I have ever witnessed, the only battlefield I ever trod while the battle was raging.... And certainly there is not the fight recorded in Concord history, at least, if in the history of America, that will bear a moment's comparison with this, whether for the members engaged in it, or for the patriotism and heroism displayed" (*Ibidem* 201).

The Walden Pond and the other ponds seem to have attracted the special attention of Thoreau, as he had selected that spot for his experimentation. He watches the peculiar beauty of the White Pond, Flint's Pond, Goose Pond and Walden Pond with deep interest and curiosity. The survey of the geographical details of the Walden Pond is quite factual: "The shore is composed of a belt of smooth rounded white stones like paving-stones, excepting one or two short sand beaches…" (*Ibidem* 162). But Thoreau is not interested only in the matter of fact details of Nature, but he derives a philosophical lesson, for example, when he says that "…of all the characters I have known, perhaps Walden wears best, and best preserves its purity. Many men have been likened to it, but few deserve that honor" (*Ibidem* 174). Sometimes he expresses his heart-felt joy in a metaphorical language: "A lake is the landscape's most beautiful and expressive feature. It is earth's eye; looking into which the beholder measures the depth of his own nature. The fluviatile trees next the shore are the slender eyelashes which fringe it, and the wooded hills and cliffs around are its overhanging bows" (*Ibidem* 163). Likewise Thoreau watches the winter and the spring with equal attention.

Thoreau's stay in the midst of Nature helped him not only to watch the details with a scientific curiosity and enjoy its beauty, but also to discover the higher, i.e. metaphysical or spiritual principles of life. That is how he rises from the almost pantheistic level to the transcendental level. He, who began his life in the woods as an experimenter, finally ends up as a mystic. A few major aspects of his spiritual discovery may be examined here. His reduction of the bodily needs helped him enrich his spiritual life: "Though the results were bodily weakness, yet perhaps no one can say that the consequences were to be regretted, for these were a life in conformity to higher principles. If the day and the night are such that you greet him with joy, and life emits a fragrance like flowers and sweet-scented herbs, is more elastic, more starry, more immortal,—that is your success…. The true harvest of my daily life is somewhat as intangible and indescribable as the tints of morning. It is a little stardust caught, a segment of the rainbow I have clutched" (*Ibidem* 194-95). The spiritual awakening and the consequent joy of life are the most valuable gains for Thoreau. The spiritual awakening involves the concurrent negation of the animalistic tendencies in man. That is why he declares, "We are conscious of an animal in us, which awakens in proportion as our higher nature slumbers" (*Ibidem* 196). True to his own dictum, Thoreau has been successful in conquering the animal in him thereby achieving a spiritual enrichment for himself. When the sanctity of the inner spirit is recognized, it is but natural for man to be charged with the divine energy. He ceases to be a brute and tends to become a mobile temple. Thoreau explains it beautifully: "Every man is a builder of a temple, called his body, to the god he worships, after a style purely his own, nor can he get off by hammering marble instead. We are all sculptors and painters, and our material is our own flesh and blood and bones. Any nobleness begins at once to refine a man's features, any meanness or sensuality to imbrute them" (*Ibidem* 199).

Thoreau's observation of the external world and his meditation about it teaches him the lesson of the essential unity of life. A realization of the unity of the world makes further observation of the external world by means of travel redundant. That is the reason why he makes a jocular remark that "It is not worth the while to go round the world to count the cats in Zanzibar" (*Ibidem* 287). He advises man to "be expert in home cosmography" (*Ibidem* 286). He points out how every man is a spiritual adventurer to explore the glory and grandeur of his own soul: "...be a Columbus to whole new continents, not of trade, but of thought. Every man is the lord of a realm beside which the earthly empire of the Czar is but a petty state, a hummock left of the ice" (*Ibidem* 286).

Thoreau's observation of Nature enables him not only to enjoy its beauty like a poet, but also to have a sort of mystic experience like a saint. Walden, for Thoreau, represents the eternity of art. It "represents a state of unchanging perfection comparable to Blake's Jerusalem, Keats's Grecian Urn, and Yeats's Byzantium" (R.W. Desai 8). Nature, thus, ceases to be just a material phenomenon, but gives him a glimpse of Divinity and an experience of ecstasy. He recounts it as follows: "Once it chanced that I stood in the very abutment of a rainbow's arch, which filled the lower strata of the atmosphere, tinging the grass and leaves around, and dazzling me as if I looked through colored crystal. It was a lake of rainbow light in which, for a short while, I lived like a dolphin. If it had lasted longer it might have tinged my employment and life" (*Ibidem* 182). Thoreau has not only the mystic experience, but also the scholarship to relate it to similar experiences had by other great people of the world: "As I walked on the railroad causeway, I used to wonder at the halo of light around my shadow, and would fain fancy myself one of the elect. One who visited me declared that the shadows of some Irishmen before him had no halo about them, that it was only natives that were so distinguished. Benvenuto Cellini tells us in his memoirs, that after a certain terrible dream or vision which he had during his confinement in the castle of St. Angelo a resplendent light appeared over the shadow of his head at morning and evening, whether he was in Italy or France, and it was particularly conspicuous when the grass was moist with dew. This was probably the same phenomenon to which I have referred, which is especially observed in the morning, but also at other times, and even by moonlight. Though a constant one, it is not commonly noticed…" (*Ibidem* 182). Thoreau has grown to the level of a mystic by noticing uncommon quality in the common things of the world. It holds mirror to the extraordinary and extrasensory perception, which is so common among the mystics of the world.

One of the advantages of Thoreau's stay in the woods was the leisure to read the classics of world literature and perceive their essential unity, in spite of apparent cultural differences among them. Reading of classics helped him to intensify his spiritual pursuits. His quotation from Mir Cama Uddin Mast is obviously in tune with his own belief: "Being seated, to run through the region of the spiritual world; I have had this advantage in books. To be intoxicated by a single glass of wine; I have experienced this pleasure when I have drunk the liquor of the esoteric doctrines" (*Ibidem* 90). One thing especially noticeable is that Thoreau was interested in reading not ordinary books, but only or mainly classics: "For what are the classics but noblest recorded thoughts of man? They are the only oracles, which are not decayed, and there are such answers to the most modern inquiry in them as Delphi and Dodona never gave…. To read well, that is, to read true books in a true spirit is a noble exercise, and one that will task the reader more than any exercise, which the customs of the day esteem. It requires training such as the athletes underwent the steady intention of almost of the whole life to this object. Books must be read as deliberately and reservedly as they were written" (*Ibidem* 92). Thoreau is very serious about the discipline of reading because of his firm faith in the exercise of reading as a means of sublimation of one's feelings: "Those, who have not learned to read the ancient classics in the language in which they were written, must have a very imperfect knowledge of the history of human race…. That age will be rich indeed when those relics which we call classics, and the still older and more than classic but even less known scriptures of the nations, shall have still further accumulated, when the Vaticans shall be filled with *Vedas* and *Zendavesta* and *Bibles*, with Homers and Dantes and Shakespeare, and all the centuries to come shall have successfully deposited their trophies in the forum of the world. By such a pile we may hope to scale heaven at last" (*Ibidem* 94). One may easily see the eclectic approach of Thoreau to knowledge and his eagerness to decipher the universals in various cultural constructs called classics. He rightly but jocularly points out the great responsibility of a reader in understanding the meaning of the text when he says that "It is not all books that are as dull as their readers" (*Ibidem* 98). He had a special fascination for all the major classics of the world. He, for example, had read Manu's *Dharma Sastra*, the *Visnu Purana*, the *Bhagavadgita*, Kalidasa's *Sakuntala* (misspelled as *Sacontala*), Vyasa's the *Mahabharata*, Homer's the *Illiad* and the *Odyssey*, the *Harivamsa*, the *Gulisthan*, the *Anaelects* of Confucius very deeply and quotes lines from them at appropriate occasions.

Some of Thoreau's ideas are comparable to Gandhi's especially regarding the rural-oriented culture and education of people. For example, Thoreau asks the right question, "Shall the world be confined to one Paris or one Oxford forever? Cannot students be boarded here and get a liberal education under the skies of Concord? Can we not hire some Abelard ro lecture to us?" (*Ibidem* 98-99). His views are obviously parallel to those of Gandhi and Rabindranath Tagore. His concept of open education is easily comparable to Tagore's concept of the Shantiniketan University at Calcutta. The enormous significance of his views on village-centred education may be seen in his opinion, which is as follows:

> New England can hire all the wise men in he world to come and teach her, and board them round the while, and not be provincial at all. That is the uncommon school we want. Instead of noblemen, let us have noble villagers of men. (*Ibidem* 100)

Thoreau has been experimenting with living alone near the Walden Pond like a real *vanaprastha*. Living in the woods faraway from the madding crowd of the city give man a great opportunity for the obseration of Nature, which is a manifestation of the Divine Principle and meditaion about the spiritual values of life. Thoreau sounds exactly like an Hindu yogi when he realizes the Hindu way of life. "I realized what the Orientals mean by contemplation and the forsaking of words. For the most part, I minded not how the hours went" (*Ibidem* 102). He continues to say, "I lived like the Puri Indians, of whom it is said that 'for yesterday, today, and tomorrow they have only one word, and they express the variety of meaning by pointing backward for yesterday, forward for tomorrow, and overhead for the present day'" (*Ibidem* 102).

Thoreau believes in the dignity of physical work and does not depend upon servants to do any menial job for him. That shows his true greatness. It is quite in line with Basaveswara's (a twelfth century super saint from Karnataka, India) concept of *kayaka*, which recognizes the holiness and dignity of all work, physical or mental. Thoreau not only preaches this principle implicitly but actually practises it on the Walden Pond. For example his description shows his actual accomplishment, "Housework was a pleasant pastime. When my floor was dirty, I rose early, and setting all my furniture out of doors on the grass, bed and bedstead making but one budget, dashed water on the floor, and sprinkled white sand from the pond on it, and then with a broom scrubbed it clean and white; and by the time the villagers had broken their fast the morning sun had dried my house sufficiently to allow me to move in again, and my meditations were almost uninterrupted" (*Ibidem* 102-03).

Thoreau has reserved one whole chapter for the sounds of various kinds on the Walden Pond. He has a keen eye for the sights and sounds of Nature around him. He describes the various plants and creepers around his hut with almost a scientist's microscopic precision and interest: "My house was on the side of a hill, immediately on the edge of the larger wood, in the midst of a young forest of pitch pines and hickories, and half a dozen rods from the pond, to which a narrow footpath led down the hill. In my front yard grew the strawberry, blackberry, and life-everlasting, johnswort and goldenrod, shrub oaks and sand cherry, bluberry and groundnut. Near the end of May, the sand cherry adorned the sides of the path with its delicate flowers arranged in umbels cyclindrically about its short stems, which last, in the fall, weighed down with good-sized and handsome cherries, fell over in wreathes like rays on every side. I tasted them out of compliment to Nature, though they were scarcely palatable" (*Ibidem* 103). Likewise he refers to sumach and other trees and describes their details almost microscopically like a scientist. Although Thoreau was a layman, he has described these details of flora almost like a scientist, especially a botanical scientist. One wonders whether such details are or can ever be described by an Indian author. I have not seen any Indian author describing nature so minutely as Thoreau does. His depiction of Nature is almost photographic, which is not possible for anyone unless he or she has remarkable powers of observation and the right kind of vocabulary to articulate the experience.

Thoreau has heard a variety of sounds produced by Nature and by man-made world. Again he has exhibited his remarkable powers or auditory sensibility in hearing different sounds, melodies and songs that are available in life. For example he has recorded the various sounds produced by birds like hawks (tantivy of), wild pigeons, sedge and reed-birds, etc. He listens to these sounds with a child-like curiosity: "...for the last half hour I have heard the rattle of railroad cars, now dying away and then reviving like he beat of a partridge, conveying travellers from Boston to the country" (*Ibidem* 104). Onc may casily scc a poct's sensibility in Thoreau's audition of these sounds and melodies of Nature. For example he says, "The whistle of the locomotive penetrates my woods summer and winter, sounding like the scream of a hawk sailing over some farmer's yard, informing me that many restless city merchants are arriving within the circle of the town, or adventurous country traders from the other side" (*Ibidem* 105). The sounds and sights of the earthly life instantly bring in the connections with the celestial world in Thoreau's mind. For example he says, "I watch the passage of the morning cars with the same feeling that I do the rising of the sun, which is hardly more regular. Their train of clouds stretching far behind and rising higher and higher, going to heaven while the cars are going to Boston, conceals the sun for a minute and cast my distant field into the shade, a celestial train beside which the petty train of cars which hugs the earth is but the barb of the spear" (*Ibidem* 106). Thus the earthly things and events instantly awaken in him an unearthly associations thereby turning him into a poet as well as a saint.

He has the habit of describing their sounds in an appropriate manner. For example, "When other birds are still, the screech owls take up the strain, like mourning women their ancient *ululu*. Their dismal scream is truly Ben Jonsonian. Wise midnight hags! It is no honest and blunt tu-whit-tu-who of the poets, but, without jesting, a most solemn graveyard ditty, the mutual consolations of suicide lovers remembering the pangs and the delights of supernal love in the infernal groves. Yet I love to hear their wailing, their doleful responses, trilled along the woodside; reminding me sometimes of music and singing birds; as if it were the dark and tearful side of music, the regrets and sighs that would be fain be sung. They are the spirits, the low spirits and melancholy forebodings, of fallen souls that once in human shap night walked the earth and did the deeds of darkness, now expiating their sins with their wailing hymns or thronodies in the scenery of their transgressions" (*Ibidem* 113). He enjoys every sound or song of every bird like a true yogi, who considers the entire universe as a manifestation of God and hears the Divine voice in this multiplicity of sounds, songs and voices of Nature. For example he says, "I rejoice that there are owls. Let them do the idiotic and maniacal hooting for men" (*Ibidem* 114). Likewise he enjoys hearing the baying of dogs, the sound of cock-drowing, wild cockerels, Blue jays, woodchuck, a screech owl and a fox, etc. Many of these birds are unknown to Indians and help them to know a great variety of birds not found in India. They enrich the ornithological knowledge of Indian readers. In this varied description of the sounds of a plurality of birds, Thoreau seems to hear the Divine Melody itself.

Referring to the incurability of human nature, Thoreau quotes an Oriental, especially Indian proverb, which shows his deep knowledge of the Oriental wisdom and thought. Referring to the Concord merchants and their evil habits, Thoreau says, "I confess, that, practically speaking, when I have learned a man's real disposition, I have no hopes of changing it for the better or worse in this state of existence. As the orientals say, 'A cur's tail may be warmed, and pressed, and found with ligatures, and after a tweve years' labor bestowed upon it, still it will retain its natural form'" (*Ibidem* 110).

It is quite obvious that Thoreau went to live near the Walden Pond to live a lonely life for the observation of Nature, simple living and deep meditation about life. Having chosen a life of loneliness, he has no reason to complaint against it. On the contrary he enjoys being lonely. For a modern man who suffers from the existential anxiety, loneliness may turn out to be a suicidal condition and a sort of psychic punishment. But for a spiritually oriented and a yogi-like man like Thoreau this loneliness comes as a blessing. It is easily termed as solitude, which is absolutely necessary for spiritual meditation. Thoreau says, "My nearest neighbor is a mile distant..." (*Ibidem* 118). Though he is alone (away from the human company), he is in the midst of the company of Nature and its cyclical seasons, "While I enjoy the friendship of the seasons I trust that nothing can make life a burden to me" (*Ibidem* 119). For him social living or gregariousness is the mark of undeveloped human beings. He says, "Society is commonly too cheap" (*Ibidem* 123). He recounts his experience of solitude and justifies it, "I find is wholesome to be alone the greater part of the time. To be in company, even with the best, is soon wearisome and dissipating. I love to be alone. I never found the companion that was so companionable as solitude. We are for the most part more lonely when we go abroad among men than when we stay in our chambers. A man thinking or working is always alone, let him be where he will" (*Ibidem* 123-24). From his individual experience Thoreau goes on to generalize about the solitude or loneliness of all geat things and beings in the universe, "I am no more lonely than the loon in the pond that laughs so loud, or than Walden Pond itself. What company has the lonely lake? I pray? And yet it has not the blue devils, but the blue angels in it, in the azure tint of its waters. The sun is alone, except in thick weather, when there sometimes appear to be two, but one is a mock sun. God is alone—but the devil, he is far from being alone; he sees a great deal of company; he is legion" (*Ibidem* 124). Thoreau does not feel lonely simply because he lives in the company of Nature, for its indescribable innocence and beneficence. He attributes the eternal youth and health of Nature to its inner energy. He therefore says, "What is the pill which will keep us well, serene, contented? Not my or thy great-grandfather's, but our great-grandmother Nature's universal, vegetable, botanic medicines, by which she has kept herself young always, outlived so many old Parrs in her day, and fed her health with their decaying fatness" (*Ibidem* 125).

***

While Thoreau lived on the bank of the Walden Pond, he had a limited number of visitors about whom he has recorded in his autobiography, "I think that I love society as much as most, and am ready enough to fasten myself like a bloodsucker for the time to any full-blooded man that comes in my way. I am naturally no hermit, but might possibly sit out the sturdiest frequenter of the bar-room, if my business called me hither" (*Ibidem* 127). Thoreau is like a yogi in his being a minimalist satisfied with the minimum requirements for a happy living. It may be seen in his minimum facilities that he had in his house, "I had three chairs in my house; one for solitude, two for friendship, three for society. When visitors came in larger and unexpected numbers there was the third chair for them all, but they generally economized the room by standing up" (*Ibidem* 127). Thoreau appreciate the large-heartedness of man rather than the large houses and mansions owned by him, which are simply superfluous, "Many of houses, both public and private, with their almost innumberable apartments, their huge halls and their cellars for the storge of wines and other munitions of peace, appear to me extravagantly large for their inhabitants. They are so vast and magnificent that the latter seem to be only vermin which infest them" (*Ibidem* 127).

Thoreau recognizes the need for the boundaries between human beings in order for them to be good neighbours. As it is said, good fences make good neighours. He says, "Individuals, like nations, must have suitable broad and natural boundaries, even a considerable neutral ground, between them. I have found it a singular luxury to talk across the pond to a companion on the opposite side" (*Ibidem* 128). He received an occasional visitor he shared his frugal meal with him but if many visitors came to meet him, he could not treat them with meals at all, but all the while he talked sweetly and sympathetically with them. Once he received a woodchopper and post-maker, who was a Homeric or Paphlagonian man with a poetic name and who was a hard worker and interested in reading books to kill his time during the rainy season. This so-called ordinary man struck as a philosopher and a prince in disguise for Thoreau. When Thoreau asked him if he wanted the world to be changed, the visitor answered with a chuckle of surprise in his Canadian accent, "No, I like it well enough" (*Ibidem* 134). Like a philosopher and a realist the visitor was quite satisfied with the world as it already is rather than complaining against it and wishing to be something different from what it is. Thus Thoreau has the capacity to discern the extraordinary qualities in the so-called ordinary human beings. He generalizes about the ordinary men as follows, "He suggested that there might be men of genius in the lowest grades of life, however permanently humble and illiterate…" (*Ibidem* 136). Likewise Thoreau saw or received many visitors like runaway slaves, paupers, girls, children, boys, young women and men of business in whom he saw some educative or ennobling quality or the other and without having or showing any contempt for anyone. But in winter he did not receive any guest although he waited eagerly for them. He believes in the Hindu practice of treating the guests as though they are gods. "The Vishnu Purana says, 'The house-holder is to remain at even tide in his courtyard as long as it takes to milk a cow, or longer if he pleases, to await the arrival of a guest.' I often performed this duty of hospitality, waited long enough to milk a whole herd of cows, but did not see the man approaching from the town" (*Ibidem* 242). He seems to have believed that everything in this world is a gift of God and part of His Divine Frolic (*Lila*) as the Hindu generally believe.

Sarvajna, the 16th century itinerant poet of Karnataka (in South India) said that the knowledge of the harvesting pillar is greater than any other knowledge in the world. The harvesting pillar is a symbol of agriculture known to all Indians. Agriculture, obviously, is the foundation of all culture, because man simply cannot survive without the food grains produced by agriculture. Karl Marx also recognized the enormous importance of agricultural production in his economic theory. Thoreau spends most of his time in agricultural work like planting the beans and other corns, potatoes, etc. Agricultural work is basically manual work. Thoreau had recognized the dignity and holiness of physical labour, which principle was parallel to Karl Marx's concept of labour and Basaveswara's concept of *kayaka*. He did not consider the manual labour as inferior to mental labour as many of moderns think. He, therefore, spent some time regularly on his farm doing the physical labour. "What was the meaning of this so steady and self-respecting, this small Herculean labor, I knew not. I came to love my rows, my beans, though so many more than I wanted. They attached me to the earth, and so I got strength like Anteaus" (*Ibidem* 140). Thus agricultural labor brought him to the Mother-Earth and made him the true son of the soil like any farmer of the world. He describes his daily work as follows: "Removing the weeds, putting fresh soil about the bean stems, and encouraging this weed which I had grown, making the yellow soil express its summer thought in bean leaves and blossoms rather than in wormwood and piper and millet grass, making the earth say beans instead of grass,—this was my daily work. As I had little aid from horses or cattle, or hired men or boys, or improved implements of husbandry, I was much slower, and became much more intimate with my beans than usual.... It has a constant and imperishable moral, and to the scholar it yields a classic result. A very *agricola laborious* was I to travellers bound westward through Lincoln and Wayland to nobody knows where" (*Ibidem* 141-42).

As we have alredy seen, Thoreau has the capacity to see some extraordinary meaning in the so-called ordinary things of life. For example, his simple agricultural task of digging the earth made him aware of the primeval history of man, "As I drew a still fresher soil about the rows with my hoe, I disturbed the ashes of unchronicled nations who in primeval years lived under these heavens, and their small implements or war and hunting were brought to the light of this modern day" (*Ibidem* 143). Obviously Thoreau has been able to discover the harmony between the past and the present; between history and contemporary life. He takes great delight in cutting the weeds in his field. Thoreau defends his love for agricultural labor in a beautiful manner, "Those summer days which some of my contemporaries devoted to the fine arts in Boston or Rome, and others to contemplation in India, and others to trade in

London or New York, I thus, with the other farmers of New England, devoted to husbandry" (*Ibidem* 146). He even gives a balance sheet of his frugal investment and humble income, but he does the work not with a profitarion motive, but with a religious sense of sanctity and dedication, which is backed up by his knowledge of ancient poetry and mythology, "Ancient poetry and mythology suggest, at least, that husbandry was once a sacred art; but it is pursued with irreverent haste and heedlesness by us, our object. Being to have large farms and large crops merely. We have no festival, nor procession, nor ceremony, not expecting our cattle-shows and so-called Thanksgivings, by which the farmer expresses a sense of the sacredness of his calling, or is reminded of its sacred origin" (*Ibidem* 149).

***

Thoreau has great liking for the village life and its simplicity. That is why he used to walk to the nearest village and watch the people with deep interest. "I observed that the vitals of the village were the grocery, the bar-room, the post-office, and the bank; and, as a necessary part of the machinery, they kept a bell, a big gun, and a fire-engine, at convenient places; and the houses were so arranged as to make the most of mankind, in lanes and fronting one another, so that every traveller had to run the gauntlet, and every man, woman, and child might get a lick at him" (*Ibidem* 152). He, like Mahatma Gandhi, appreciates the simple life of the villagers. "I am convinced, that if all men were to live as simply as I then did, thieving and robbery would be unknown. These take place only in communities where some have got more than is sufficient while others have not enough" (*Ibidem* 155-56). Thoreau's ideas are parallel to those of Basaveswara, Gandhi and Karl Marx who in different contexts uphold the virtues of non-possession and non-hoarding by the rich people. If there is no class conflict, which is economically determined there will be no problem for humanity at all. This happens to be Thoreau's utopian idea.

***

Since Thoreau lived on the shore of the Walden Pond, he has observed the other ponds in the vicinity and recorded his meticulous observation of their distinct features. Once he sat in a boat along with a fisherman and had a silent communication with him, "Our intercourse was thus altogether one of unbroken harmony, far more pleasing to remember than if it had been carried on by speech" (*Ibidem* 158). He mentions different ponds like White Pond, Flint's Pond, and Goose Pond and describes their length, irregular shores, depth, the colour of their waters, the acquatic creatures dwelling in them and their rise and fall, their purity and transparency, etc., meticulously realistically, which provide ample material for a geographer to analyse. Sometimes these descriptions tend to be tedious and hence boring also. But the boredom is compensated for by his poetic and philosophical remarks about his experiences there. His poetic sensibility may be seen in his metaphorical description of the pond, "A lake is the landscape's most beautiful and expressive feature. It is earth's eye; looking into which the beholder measures the depth of his own nature. The fluviatile trees nest to the shore are the slender eyelashes which fringe it, and the wooded hills and cliffs around are its overhanging brows" (*Ibidem* 168). His metaphorical talent may be seen in his description of these ponds, "White Pond and Walden are great crystals on the surface of the earth, Lakes of Light" (*Ibidem* 180).

***

While visiting the pine trees near the Baker Farm Thoreau rambles in the pine groves. His comparison of the tall pine trees to temples and pagodas shows his deep religious orientation and fine poetic sensibility. Once he had a romantic experience of standing at the edge of a rainbow, which borders on the ethereal and the mystic experience, "Once it chanced that I stood in the very abutment of a rainbow's arch, which filled the lower stratum of the atmosphere, tinging the grass and leaves around, and dazzling me as if I looked through coloured crystal. It was a lake of rainbow light, in which, for a short while, I lived like a dolphin" (*Ibidem* 182). Thoreau had a strange experience of having a halo around his shadow and compares its similar experience that Benvenuto Cellini had in Italy or France. Obviously, this halo, although it might be generated due to geographical factors, has a religious and occult associations about it. Every experience should be invigorating and enlightening and educative for Thoreau. That is why he says, "We should come home from far, from adventures, and perils, and discoveries every day, with new experience and character" (*Ibidem* 188).

***

In the earlier chapter Thoreau has shown the contrast between John Field and himself. Whereas John Field ate heavy food and had to work hard to acquire it, Thoreau says he ate simple food and did not have to struggle hard to get it. Thoreau is obviously a spiritually-oriented man, as the Indian reader can easily discern it. This is corroborated by Thoreau's confession, "I found myself, and till find, an instinct towards a higher, or, as it is named, spiritual life, so do most men, and another towards a primitive rank and savage one, and I reverence them both. I love the wild not less than the good" (*Ibidem* 189). Perhaps the quintessence of his religious-philosophical worldview is expressed in the chapter on "Higher Laws". He has a capacity to see the extraordinary in the ordinary, the supernatural in the natural and the metaphysical in the physical reality. Like Mahatma Gandhi he pleads for the vegetarian food on the grounds of cleanliness and purity. "I have found repeatedly, of late years, that I cannot eat fish without fling a little in self-respect.... The practical objection to animal food in my case was its uncleanness; and besides, when I had caught and cleaned and cooked and eaten my fish, they seemed not have fed me essentially. It was insignificant and unnecessary, and cost me more than it came to" (*Ibidem* 192-93). Like Hindus, Thoreau sees the connection between vegetarian food and higher faculties of man. "It appeared more beautiful to live low and fair hard in many respects; and though I never did so, I went far enough to please my imagination. I believe that every man who has ever been earnest to preserve his higher or poetic faculties in the best condition has been particularly inclined to abstain from animal food, and from much food of any kind" (*Ibidem* 193). Just as Thoreau is against non-vegetarian food, he is against alcoholism also. He pleads for the use of water as a common drink for man, "I believe that water is the only drink for a wise man; wine is not so noble a liquor" (*Ibidem* 195).

Thoreau considers Nature as a source of bliss when he says, "All Nature is your congratulations, and you have cause momentarily to bless yourself" (*Ibidem* 195). This view is easily comparable to Basaveswara's view that everything including the earth, the blowing wind and the abundant crop growing on the earth is the gift of God to Man. According to Hindu philosophy, the entire world is a work of art for a yogi, who experiences mystic bliss in the enjoyment of this divine work of art. Thoreau has the same experience. As he says, "The true harvest of my daily life is somewhat as intangible and indescribable as the tints of morning or evening. It is a little star-dust caught, segment of the rainbow which I have clutched" (*Ibidem* 195).

Being a morally awakened man, Thoreau sees some moral or the other in everything that he sees or does, "We cannot touch a string or move a stop but the charming moral transfixes us. Many an irksome noise, go a long way off, is heard as music, a proud, sweet satire on the meanness of our lives" (*Ibidem* 197). Thoreau's ideas are parallel to the universal ideas of the mystics, philosophers and religious visionaries. We know that man is a combination of the angel and the devil and that one grows powerful in proportion as the other grows weak. The same principle is articulated by Thoreau here, "We are conscious of an animal in us, which awakens in proportion as our higher nature slumbers" (*Ibidem* 197). He pays tribute to the Hindu philosophy which pleads for the self-control of man. "A command over our passions, and over the external senses of the body, and good acts, are declared by the *Ved* to be indispensable in the mind's approximation to God" (*Ibidem* 197). Further he recognizes the inter-relatedness of all virtues required for a harmonious life of man. For example he defines chastity which manifests in various other virtues also of man, "Chastity is the flowering of man; and what are called Genius, Heroism, Holiness and the like, are but various fruits which succeed it. Man flows at once to God when the channel of purity is open" (*Ibidem* 197). Just as there is a unity among the virtues, there is also a unity among the vices of man. Thoreau, therefore, says, "All sensuality is one, though it takes many forms; all purity is one. It is the same whether a man eat, or drink, or cohabit, or sleep sensually" (*Ibidem* 198).

Cleanliness and holiness are inseparably connected in the Hindu tradition, which is codified by Manu in his classic *Dharma Sastra*. Man should take care of every act of his, no matter how big or small it is. Thoreau expresses his regard to Manu when he quotes from the latter, "In earlier ages, in some countries, every function was reverently spoken of and regulated by law. Nothing was too trivial for the Hindoo lawgiver, however offensive, it may be, to modern taste. He teaches how to eat, drink, cohabit, void excrement and urine, and the like, elevating what is mean, and does not falsely excuse himself by calling these things trifles" (*Ibidem* 199).

Basaveswara, a super *sarana* of twelfth-century Karnataka in India rebelled against the brahmanical tradition of building temples for gods and thereby breeding a variety of evils including exploitation by the priestly class and the temple-prostitution. Instead of building temples for gods, he pleaded that every man should convert his own person into a moving temple and put an end to the temple-culture with all its attendant evils. It is indeed marvellous that even Thoreau, an American (Americans are generally notorious for their crass materialism and promiscuity) has expressed similar ideas about the need for the divinization of the human person. He says, "Every man is the builder of a temple, called his body, to the god he worships, after a style purely his own, nor can he get off by hammering marble instead. We are all sculptors and painters, and our material is our own flesh and blood and bones. Any nobleness begins at once to refine a man's features, any meanness or sensuality to imbrute them" (*Ibidem* 199).

Thoreau is a meticulous observer and recorder of his experience of living in the midst of Nature, including its flora and fauna and other beautiful aspects of it. It is said that he was deeply interested in the botanical study of Nature. Hence his description of the details of Nature are very precise and specific. But in spite of his realistic and almost photographic descriptions, sometimes he reaches the poetic heights when he makes memorable philosophical observations about them. In his flight from the mundane to the ethereal he almost reminds us of Wordsworthian ventures. He describes birds (like phoebe, robin, partridge, otter, racoon, woodcock, turtle doves, loon, geese), animals (like cats, dogs, beasts, flowers), fruits (like blackberry, cranberry, , chestnuts, ground-nuts) trees, (like maples aspens), insects (like wasps), creepers, which are typical American and hence not familiar to Indians. His description of the battle of ants is really microscopic and poetic. In this battle of ants, Thoreau sees an echo of the human wars and the their fight for some principle or the other, "Thy fought with more pertinacity than bulldogs. Neither manifested the least dispostion to retreat. It was evident that their battle-cry was 'Conquer or die'.... And certainly there is not the fight recorded in Concord history; at least, if in the history of America, that will bear a moment's comparison with this, whether for the numbers engaged in it, or for the patriotism and heroism displayed. For numbers and for carnage it was an Austerlitz or Dresden. Concord Fight!... I have no doubt that it was a principle they fought for, as much as our ancestors" (*Ibidem* 206-07). Similarly he describes the beauty of water bubbles, their freezing and bursting in the pond meticulously and realistically.

Thoreau's description of his building a simple house for himself and living in it reminds us of the Hindu ascetics' stay in the *ashrams* in the forest. He thus becomes a forest philosopher of America meditating on life.

His observation of the Walden and other ponds in different seasons in its various moods shows different meanings to him. Water and pond may be said to have archetypal, philosophical as well as psychological meanings according to our perspectives. Water shows the origin of human life. According to Freud the human foetus will be floating in the water of mother's womb. Water is a cleansing and purifying instrument for medical and religious purposes. It may stand for the depth of man's character, for the beauty of objects and transparency and dynamism and so on and so forth. Thoreau has seen different meanings of life in the ponds that he has observed during his stay in this region. We have already observed how Thoreau leaps from physics to metaphysics, from

Nature to supernatural, from the empirical to the transcendental levels of understanding. He is himself conscious of this thought process when he says, "What I have observed of the pond is no less true in ethics. It is the law of the average. Such a rule of the two diameters not only guides us towards the sun in the system and the heart in man, but draw lines through the length and breadth of the aggregate of a man's particular daily behaviours and waves of life into his coves and inlets, and where they intersect will be the height or depth of his character. Perhaps we need only to know how his shores trend and his adjacent country or circumstances, to infer his depth and concealed bottom" (*Ibidem* 260). Thoreau shows the difference between emotions and intellect by giving a comparison between the frozen water and the flowing or freely moving water, "Why is it that a bucket of water soon becomes putrid, but frozen remains sweet forever? It is commonly said that this is the difference between the affections and the intellect" (*Ibidem* 265).

At other moments the Walden Pond becomes the symbol of his eclectic philosophy recognizing the unity of all life and spiritual elevation and bliss. Obviously Thoreau scales the height of a poet, mystic and philosopher when he makes this wonderful observation, "Thus it appears that the sweltering inhabitants of Charleston and New Orleans, of Madras and Bombay and Calcutta, drink at my well. In the morning I bathe my intellect in the stupendous and cosmogonal philosophy of the *Bhagavat Gita*, since whose composition years of the gods have elapsed, and in comparison with which our modern world and its literature seem puny and trivial; and I doubt if that philosophy is not to be referred to a previous state of existence, so remote is its sublimity from our conception. I lay down the book and go to my well for water, and lo! There I meet the servant of the Brahmin, priest of Brahma, Vishnu and Indra, who still sits in his temple of the Ganges reading the Vedas, or dwells at the root of a tree with his crust and water jug. I meet his servant come to draw water for his master, and our buckets as it were grate together in the same well. The pure Walden water is mingled with the sacred water of the Ganges" (*Ibidem* 266).

What is remarkable about Thoreau's stay in the woods of Walden is that his observation of the external world including Nature, people and the cosmic world sooner or later lead him to the inner world of the self, which is in line with the Hindu philosophy and similar other ones. As Aristotle said knowing one's self is the most difficult one. As the Hindus believe the human being is the microcosm which has all the principles and laws of the macrocosm represented in it qualitatively. All external adventure and exploration should lead one to the inner world.

This is exactly what has happened to Thoreau. In support of this view he quotes a poem which says,

Direct your eye right inward, and you'll find
A thousand regions in your mind
Yet undiscovered. Travel them, and be
Expert in home-cosmography. (*Ibidem* 286)

He expresses the same idea in his own way with several examples, Nay, be Columbus, to whole new continents and worlds within you, opening new channels, not of trade, but of thought. Every man is the lord of a realm beside which the earthly empire of the Czar is but a petty state, a hummock felt by the ice" (*Ibidem* 286). A man, like a yogi, who can explore the inner world need not bother about the physical travel in the external world. That is why Thoreau observes, "It is not worth the while to go round the world to count the cats in Zanzibar" (*Ibidem* 187) Having shown the futility of physical travel he clearly states, "Explore thyself" (*Ibidem* 287). He shows how as man advances in his spiritual meditation and contemplation by practising simplicity of living, he discovers the higher laws. "In proportion as he simplifies his life, the laws of the universe will appear less complex, and solitude will not be solitude, nor poverty poverty, nor weakness weakness. If you have built castles in the air, your work need not be lost; that is where they should be. Now put the foundations under them (*Ibidem* 288).

Thoreau teaches man to have the existential courage to be, that he should face life boldly, "However mean your life is, meet it and live it; do not shun it and call it hard names. It is not so bad as you are. It looks poorest when you are richest. The faultfinder will find fault even in paradise. Love your life poor as it is" (*Ibidem* 292). He offers many epigrammatic suggestions to man like, "Cultivate poverty like a garden herb, like sage.... Sell your cloths and keep your thoughts.... Humility like darkness reveals the heavenly lights.... Superfluous wealth can buy superfluities only. Money is not required to buy one necessary of the soul" (*Ibidem* 292-93). He concludes his autobiography with the final obsevation about the spiritual awakening, "The light which puts out our eyes is darkness to us. Only that day dawns to which we are awake. There is more day to dawn. The sun is but a morning star" (*Ibidem* 297).The dominant imagery to be seen in the *Walden* is the gradual transition from winter into spring, which is symbolic of spiritual awakening. "The dominant metaphors of inward spring and inward morning appear constantly in many forms, emphasizing this theme" (William Drake 79). Thus *Walden* may be described as an autobioraphy of self-awakening and spiritual enlightenment through his experimental living in the forest of Boston

WORKS CITED

Desai, Rupin. W. "Walden Pond, Thoreau's Byzantium" (Unpublished article, nd).

Drake, William. "Walden," in *Thoreau: A Collection of Critical Essays*, ed. Sherman Paul, New Jersey; Prentice Hall, Inc, 1962.

Schneider, Richard J. "Walden," in *The Cambride Companion to Henry David Thoreau,* ed. Joel Myerson, Cambridge: Cambridge University Press, 1995.

Thoreau, Henry David. *Walden*. Delhi: S. Chand & Co., 1977.

❑❑❑

Statement about Ownership and other Particulars of
The Atlantic Critical Review

FORM IV (See Rule 8)

Place of Publication	:	New Delhi
Periodicity of the Publication	:	Quarterly
Printer's Name	:	Manish Kumar
Nationality	:	Indian
Address	:	B-2, Vishal Enclave, New Delhi-110027
Publisher's Name	:	Manish Kumar
Nationality	:	Indian
Address	:	B-2, Vishal Enclave, New Delhi-110027
Editor's Name	:	Mohit K. Ray
Nationality	:	Indian
Address	:	77, Green Park, Burdwan, West Bengal-713104
Names and addresses of individuals who own the newspaper and partners or shareholders holding more than one per cent of the total capital	:	K.R. Gupta B-2, Vishal Enclave New Delhi-110027

I, Manish Kumar, hereby declare that the particulars given above are true to the best of my knowledge and belief.

Sd/-

Date : 1st July, 2014

MANISH KUMAR
Publisher

Dynamics of Adaptations: A Comparative Study of the Film Version of *A Streetcar Named Desire*

SHIPRA GUPTA

"ADAPTATIONS are everywhere today: on the television and movie screen, on the musical and dramatic stage, on the internet, in novels and comic books, in your nearest theme park and video arcade" observes Linda Hutcheon in her work "Beginning to Theorize Adaptation: What? Who? Why? How? Where? When?", *A Theory of Adaptation*. It has been estimated that a third of all films ever made are adapted from novels. And if we include other forms of literature like plays, short-stories, comics, scriptures, autobiographies, etc., the number goes up to sixty-five per cent or more. Ira Konigsberg, in *The Complete Film Dictionary*, describes adaptations as "a work in one medium that derives its impulse as well as varying number of its elements from a work in a different medium". This definition can extend to a multitude of interpreted work. Adaptations are, undoubtedly, extensions or interpretations of the original story. The significance, however, doesn't end there, there's more to it than meets the eye. It started with the classical Greek playwrights who adapted myths that had travelled from generation to generation through oral tradition. These sources were used by many famous writers like Shakespeare as material for their works which were later adapted to screenplays by film-makers. Shakespeare's famous comedies like *All's Well That Ends Well, As You Like It, The Comedy of Errors*; his tragedies like *Hamlet, Julius Caesar, King Lear, Macbeth*; even histories like *Henry IV, Henry V, Henry VI, Richard II, Richard III* have all been successfully adapted to films. Also movies in other languages and in different countries have drawn inspiration from Shakespeare's plays. For example the Hindi movie *Angoor* which released in 1982 was based on Ishwar Chandra Vidyasagar's Bengali play by the same name which in turn was an adaptation of Shakespeare's *The Comedy of Errors*. In recent times we have the Indian director Vishal Bharadwaj in whose works we find the modern-day adaptations of Shakespeare's plays *Macbeth*, *Othello* and *Hamlet* in the movies *Maqbool*, *Omkara* and *Haider.*

Though the art of cinema is relatively new, old by only a hundred years or so, when compared to the approximately five-hundred-year history of printing-press culture and the thousand year histories of manuscript cultures, its development occurred in late 19th century, which attempted to minimize the role of the author in narrating, and instead use frames which allowed characters and their actions to 'speak for themselves'. Here the role of the *Frame* is very important. Frames are the boundaries within which the movement of the images are controlled in a film, so as to make the film look more appealing to the spectators; it plays an important role in forming opinions of the viewers about a particular scene. For instance, the viewers have a tendency to look at the center of the image, as to where the main action should be taking place; this idea has been reinforced by tradition that originated hundreds of years ago in paintings and drawings of the fifteenth century where the eye, unless trained otherwise, tends to seek images at the centre of the frame. If empty space exists at the centre, i.e., if the image is at the farthest corner of the frame then another image must be present in the other end as a continuation of the previous image in order to balance the frame. For instance if we see birds flying in one direction at one end of the frame, our eyes immediately move towards the center, then to the other end to see if they are flying to a tree or to food lying on the ground. But if we see the birds flying at the center of the frame we percieve them as just that, i.e., birds flying. Therefore the director and the cameraman have to keep in mind this centralizing tendency of the human brain while creating frames for particular scenes. Thus composition of the frames could be modified by the arrangement of people and objects within it. Certain directors allow objects and people to move around freely within the frame. Directors like Howard Hawks and Jean Renoir use the frame as an insufficient container, i.e., the action as taking place off-screen along with the action taking place on-screen which the camera incidentally observed. Here the events or incidents are moving past the camera instead of the camera arranging objects within the frame and creating an incident through movement within it. For example, in the movie *A Streetcar Named Desire*, the opening scene where we see Blanche arriving in New Orleans, she is just another person amongst the multitude of people going about their daily work and the camera happens to capture the routine of life in the French Quarter of New Orleans.

(Blanche's arrival in New Orleans)

Frames also help the viewer forsee certain incidents about to happen in the movie, for instance, if we observe carefully the scene where Blanche requests Mitch to put a paper lamp on the bare light bulb we find the lamp foreshadowing Mitch's face until his face is barely visible behind it even while he is conversing with Blanche. But we can see Blanche's face clearly. Thus the presence of Blanche, Mitch and the paper lamp in the same frame with Mitch's face being pushed to the background indicates the beginnings of deception by Blanche using the paper lamp as her ally to conceal her real age and her dark past.

(Mitch totally foregrounded by the paper lamp)

(Mitch's face partially hidden behind the paper lamp)

Cinema began as a source of entertainment for the proletariat who watched popular nickelodeons because they could not read or write. One contemporary survey reveals that "in 1911, 78 per cent of the New York [city] audience consisted of members from the working class" (Desmond 2006: 15). Reading, watching plays, painting and the like were some of the sources of entertainment only for the aristocracy. Therefore, adaptations from classical literary authors such as Shakespeare, Dickens, and Hugo begin to occur to attract these people who have read these authors and were interested in seeing these fictional characters, plots and worlds brought to life (Desmond 2006: 15). Some of the earliest examples of adapting literature to films are by George Melies who released two adaptations, *Cinderella*, based on *The Brothers Grimm* story, and *King John*, the first known film to be based on the works of Shakespeare. One of the most celebrated of the early adaptations is Erich Stroheim's *Greed*, an adaptation of the 1899 novel *McTeague* by Frank Norris. Every aspect of the novel was covered in great detail and the film ran to nine and a half hours, but was later cut down to four hours and is still considered one of the greatest films ever made. Hollywood frequently relies on literature as a source for potential film projects, right from the works of William Shakespeare to the works of Stephen King, most of them have been adapted to films, because these stories have built-in audiences who would like to see their favourite characters brought to life.

While discussing adaptation of texts to films, a common assumption is that adaptations rarely fulfil reader's expectations because one has to present a work running to various hundreds of pages within the standard time frame of 90 to 120 minutes. Also while reading a book, the reader can use his imagination which he fails to do while watching a film, because everyone who watches the same movie sees the same images, therefore there is no scope of imagination beyond what is shown on screen.

Thus film adaptations can be categorised as being of three types. John Desmond and Peter Hawkes provide a very clear explanation of the different types of adaptations. They are close adaptations, loose adaptations and intermediate adaptations. If the adaptation has maintained the majority of the original material then it is a close adaptation (Desmond 2006: 44). Films like *A Streetcar Named Desire* (1951) and *Harry Potter and the Sorcerer's Stone* (2001) are two such examples. These movies do not allow individuality and creativity beyond what the original author has written. When a loose adaptation comes to the screen, it throws out the majority of the source material and creates new material (Desmond 2006: 44). Francis Ford Coppola's *Apocalypse Now* (1979) is a loose adaptation of Joseph Conrad's *Heart of Darkness*. The final category, intermediate operates somewhere in the middle between the previous two categories. Thus adaptations add, delete, and maintain the essential elements of the original material (Desmond 2006: 44). Patricia Highsmith's novel, *The Talented Mr. Ripley* (1955) was adapted to the film of the same name (1999) by Anthony Minghella. The story and the plot remain true to the novel but there are rigorous variations in the theme and character development. Thus, it is considered as an intermediate adaptation.

Films do not suggest films state. Therefore at times when the movies don't present images as imagined by the viewer, he is disappointed. A screenplay does not just pull out dialogues from the pages of a book and use them for the characters, there is more to it than it appears to be; to understand and appreciate a movie, the characters' past needs to be foregrounded keeping in mind the plot or the description of the characters' thoughts which cannot be translated as dialogues. Before the 1930s, the shallow focus of the largely immobile 35 mm cameras had to be compensated for through lighting and blocking and of course the audience mostly wanted to see the stars; so, if their faces were clearly in focus, it was felt that the background could take care of itself—if it was "interesting" decor, fine; but it was usually just additional "atmosphere" (Scholes, Comeley, Klaus, Silverman 1997: 1479). Here techniques like *analepsis* (flash-back), *prolepsis* (flash-forward), *foregrounding* and *backgrounding* come into play. Some optical effects like the *dissolve*, *freeze*, a *fade-in* or a *fade-out* are also used along with camera tricks like the *close-up*. In the 1951 movie *A Streetcar Named Desire,* though we don't come across any scenes depicting a young Blanche and her life with Allan Grey, her past is revealed through flashbacks as she herself admits about it to Mitch and Stanley, and through the music of the Varsouviana Polka ending with a gunshot. However, we don't find any occurrences of flashforward in this movie. It is a very rare phenomenon to find any example of *prolepsis* in a movie unless it is a supernatural movie consisting of prophecies and predictions or a science fiction movie where travel to the future and back is possible through technology as in the movies of *Back to the Future* series or *The Star Trek* series. However the techniques of *foregrounding* and *backgrounding* have been liberally used in *A Streetcar Named Desire*. For instance, the scene where Blanche, Stanley and Stella are seated for dinner on Blanche's birthday and Stanley is eating with both his hands, making a mess on the table. Blanche and Stella are in the background and the camera focuses on the food on Stanley's hands which has been foregrounded. Stanley represents the dominating male and the patriarchal society of that era, and Blanche on the other hand stands for the fading southern genteel. Thus, on being referred to as greasy, polack and pig, Stanley asserts his dominance by turning violent and throwing the cutlery off the table, while Blanche and Stella cower timidly and say nothing. This scene and the one foregrounding Stanley with his primitive table-manners, warns the audience of the impending doom and the final downfall of the southern aristocracy that was signified by Blanche. We also find Blanche's hysterical expression foregrounded throughout the movie with a close-up shot making clear the agitated state of her mind. The lighting and the shadows added to the ambience highlighting her nervousness even further. And this technique of deep-focus and foregrounding added depth to the scenes.

Optical effects like the *dissolve* also became very popular during those times. In order to make a scene more expressive, prominent and effective the film-maker uses this technique. A *dissolve* superimposes one image on another; the time taken to effect the transition may be brief, or it may be slowed down so much that one image remains fully visible while another is superimposed upon it (a *lap* [short for "overlapping"] *dissolve*). The image can *fade* so that the frame contains momentarily a blankness that may be either light or dark; similarly, an image may

(Stanley's table-manners highlighted)

be made (quickly or slowly) to emerge from this blankness (a *fade in* as opposed to a *fade out*) (Scholes, Comeley, Klaus, Silverman 1997: 1468). We can take an example from the movie *A Streetcar Named Desire* where Mitch finally confronts Blanche about her past and refuses to marry her but tries to kiss her as a result of which Blanche threatens him and gives out a hysterical scream alarming the neighbours. Panic-stricken with the crowd gathered around her house she runs back inside. There is a brief *dissolve* and the blankness is dark after which the *fade-in* shows a beautifully dressed Blanche dancing to an imaginary tune with an imaginary suitor. This takes us to the next set of events and the final confrontation between Blanche and Stanley.

(Blanche dancing with an imaginary suitor)

(A delusional Blanche conversing with an imaginary suitor)

A *dissolve* also symbolises the passage of time in months or in years where after a *fadeout*, the viewers find the accompanying scene as showing the characters as grown old or a change in the season or a change in the general scene as we find in *A Streetcar Named Desire* after Blanche's rape by Stanley. We notice that some time has passed and the men are at their poker game as usual. But we understand the passage of time by the presence of Stanley and Stella's baby. This is the end of Blanche because she has completely lost her sanity and has withdrawn herself into her make-believe world of yachts, cruises on the Caribbean and the fictitious admirer Shep Huntleigh. But in reality she is being sent to an insane asylum. Sometimes a dissolve may be accompanied by an illustrative symbol like whirling leaves, pages of a calendar, snowfall, a short line informing us of the date and place or directly the number of years passed to show the passage of time.

While adapting a movie, the set-design and the special effects have to be of such quality that would convince the audience and fascinate them as well. Here the skills of the artist as well as of the technician are of utmost importance because only if the cast and crew are in sync with each other, will a scene look convincing and real. Film-making is a collaborative effort unlike writing a novel or a play which solely depends on the writer and his creativity. The writer creates characters, places and situations which are brought to life by the participation and effort of the director and the cast and crew for the film.

While discussing the techniques of film-making, an important aspect that needs to be taken into account is how far does the allegiance of the film version to the original written work lie? The film-maker may also bring about certain changes while adapting a literary text to film in accordance with the demands of the new medium. George Bluestone, one of the first critics to study film adaptations of literature, believes that the film-maker is an adept artist, "not a translator for an established author, but a new author in his own right". Some people agree to it while others, however, believe that it would be letting down the original work. There are many reasons why a film-maker chooses to bring about changes: the non-availability of advanced techniques, disapproval of the censor board, experimenting with new themes, providing a solution to a problem as described in a book, emphasizing different dimensions to a particular character, or catering to the general public taste or opinion. For example, Elia Kazan's movie *A Streetcar Named Desire* adapted from the play by Tennessee Williams with the same name, posed a real challenge for the film-maker because of the limited techniques available during that era. The black and white cinematography should be given all the credit because, despite the drawback of not having colour images in a film which relies heavily on colour play, the film was a huge hit. It won twelve academy award nominations and was well received and critically acclaimed. Kazan played up the claustrophobia of the two bedroom Kowalski apartment by using walls that were actually movable, so that he could move them closer from one scene to the next, so as to make the apartment look more cramped and confined as if closing in on the characters, thus heightening the feeling of anxiety in the protagonist, Blanche. The lighting effects also play a major role in the film; one can see the lights blinking from the nearby shops inside the Kowalski apartment which makes the audience aware of the proximity of the street to the apartment. The apartment has two rooms separated by a curtain; there are no doors in the house except for the door at the entrance and a door to the bathroom. Sound of the trains passing in the neighbourhood, cats screeching, people shouting at each other, could all be heard inside the apartment. All these props intensify the congested atmosphere of the French Quarter that Kazan successfully created.

The film's comparably adult themes meant that it would run into trouble with the censor board and the question whether it would conform to the rules as laid down by them. The board demanded that certain scenes needed to be altered keeping in mind the moral sentiments of the viewers. They were: the suggestion that Blanche's husband, Allan Grey, was a homosexual; the promiscuity of Blanche; and the rape scene. Kazan had no problems with the first two, her husband was referred to as 'weak' and Blanche's past affairs suggested the need for love and companionship instead of sexual pleasure. He didn't, however, agree to alter the rape scene because it was central to the script as it suggested the final downfall of the southern genteel world, symbolized by Blanche DuBois.

Films speak differently to people who are visually literate and can hear and see more than the people who rarely go to the movies. Therefore the scene depicting Blanche's rape is shot in such a way so as to have a harrowing impact on the viewers. We get a hint of her impending doom through the scene where Stella accidentally drops alcohol on Blanche's skirt which makes her let out a frantic scream and when Stella asks her to pat it dry 'gently', she keeps repeating the word 'gently' over and over again. After it is dried Stella asks her whether the skirt got stained, Blanche replies nervously "No, not a bit!" Her skirt symbolises her stained character which she is trying to clean off, only to be scarred for life by being raped by Stanley later. It is pertinent to note here that the Kazan uses certain techniques such as cracking of the mirror with Blanche's reflection on it, faraway jungle noises playing, the tempo of the music rising and getting louder with every passing second, the menacing expression on Stanley's face while he approaches Blanche, the panic in Blanche's eyes, the wall becoming transparent, all these props and techniques enrich the scene. It was picturised thus, because the censor board wouldn't allow anything to be shown explicitly. However, only a visually literate person will be able to make out from the scene that the rape highlights the end of Blanche's sexual and mental self-esteem.

(Stanley's menacing expression just before raping Blanche)

(The panic in Blanche's eyes)

(Blanche's reflection on the shattered mirror)

Thus, part of people's ability to interpret still and moving images depends on learning: anyone can 'see' a film, but only a few can 'perceive' the visual images. Interpretation of a film means deciphering the various layers of meaning and perceiving them significantly. Only a viewer can do something to or with a film text which is dormant until then. He can observe the movie critically and ascertain facts. For example, the scene from *A Streetcar Named Desire* that dramatizes the rape of Blanche, Elia Kazan did not compromise, when the censor board suggested editing that scene, because it represented the symbolic downfall of the old south genteel which was epitomized by Blanche. Hence, to prevent the scene from appearing to be obscene, Kazan heightened the use of imagery and symbolic devices to foreground social realities and psychological disturbances. The presence of frightening, menacing and sinister shadows and reflections on the walls and the rising tempo of the music had to be captured to present the ravishment of the tender by the brutal forces of the modern world. Kazan played up the apocalyptic experience by presenting the back wall of the Kowalski apartment as becoming transparent and revealing the neighbourhood. This symbolises that one isn't safe even in the confines of a loved one's home. Then the jungle voices swell as Stanley advances towards Blanche. Finally the pulsing music indicates that Blanche is being raped by him which symbolizes the shattering of Blanche's fantasy world.

> I don't want realism! Yes, yes magic! I try to give that to people. I misrepresent things to them. I don't tell the truth, I tell what ought to be the truth. And if that is sinful, then let me be damned for it!—don't turn the light on!
>
> (*A Streetcar Named Desire*, scene 9, l. 43)

Her fear of the strong light indicates not only her hesitance from showing her face that would reveal her real age, rather, her refusing to look at the world in harsh light herself. Speaking from post-modern perspective, this movie lacks certain advanced techniques of visual effects. Most of the action takes place on the first floor of the two bedroom Kowalski apartment, except for a few scenes. The set design was such that the audience could also see 'outside' and observe characters like Steve and Eunice Hubbel, the old woman selling flowers, people walking down the road, etc. in the neighbourhood. The sound effects, the dim lighting and the men sweating inside the house while playing poker also make the apartment seem cramped and confined, heightening the feeling of a symbolic combat zone. The sounds are the never soothing noises of the past and the present; the old and the new; sounds like a cat screeching, trains passing close by, faraway gunshot which ends the varsouviana polka, the woman selling flowers for the dead appearing and re-appearing when she is most vulnerable, once, when Mitch abandoned her and next when she is threatened by Stanley; all these have a harrowing impact on Blanche. The graphic content, i.e. the depiction of sex and violence jolts the audience as well. We feel a bit traumatized after 'watching' the rape of Blanche when compared to 'reading' about it. Though it has been described in great detail by Williams with the apt use of symbols and colour imagery, the film images bother us more because of the explicit presentation of the disturbing elements which contributes to the eerie feeling. Stanley, with whom we empathized in the beginning of the play, seems repulsive towards the end because of his actions and we sympathise with Blanche. He has taken advantage of a destitute lady who is in her most fragile state of mind, and he at his triumphant best, because he is going to have a baby. The audience had high expectations from the film version because the play had come from the pen of Tennessee Williams and its Broadway release had been very successful and had earned it a Pulitzer Prize. The movie lived up to their expectations despite the limitations in film-making during that era.

Another aspect that is central to the movie is the use of signs and codes in it. Roland Barthes, in *Mythologies,* coined the terms denotation and connotation that represent two levels of signification. Denotation refers to the literal relationship between the sign and its referent, and connotation refers to the second order of meanings that are culturally encoded in the denotative meaning. In connotation, signs operate as myth makers by crystallizing abstract concepts and they make sense of the cultures that people live in (Hayward 2001: 83). *A Streetcar Named Desire* is full of denotations and connotations: the varsouviana polka that haunts Blanche denotes her past; it reminds her of the death of her husband Allan Grey who shot himself when he couldn't take the humiliation of being discovered by his wife that he was a homosexual.

In the first scene Blanche says she rode a streetcar named Desire, then transferred to one called Cemeteries, which brought her to a street called Elysian Fields. This journey is connotative of Blanche's journey towards destruction and her subsequent descent to madness. The Elysian Fields are the land of the dead in Greek Mythology. Thus Blanche's promiscuity and affairs allegorically lead her to destruction and death. Further it is to be noted that Tennessee Williams uses certain mythological, symbolic and metaphorical devices that contribute to the development of the plot and its characters:

> They told me to take a street-car named desire, and then transfer to one called Cemeteries and ride six blocks and get off at—Elysian Fields!
>
> (*A Streetcar Named Desire*, scene 1, l. 16)

Film is a sequence of signs and codes therefore the importance of an object portrayed on screen doesn't depend on one shot alone, rather it depends on those presented before and after the shot. For instance, the scene after the rape of Blanche depicts the road being washed out of the dirt lying there from the previous night with a close-up shot of the water coming out with full force. This shot denotes that water can remove superficial dirt but no amount of water can purge the tarnished soul. This scene *rhymes* with Blanche's constant bathing throughout the film.

(The shot immediately after Blanche's rape, of the jet of water clearing the dirt off the roads)

Films carry both denotative and connotative meanings. Though an image of a person or an object has a denotative dimension, all images are culturally charged by connotative procedures available in cinema such as camera angle or position, usage of light, sound, colour process and the way people and objects are framed; the mirror cracking and the quick fade-out denotes rape; the varsouviana polka ending with the gunshot are sounds of horror for Blanche.

"Blanche: Something's the matter tonight, but never mind. I won't cross-examine the witness. I'll just [*She touches her forehead vaguely. The polka tune starts up again*]—pretend I don't notice anything different about you.

That—music again-

Mitch: What music?

Blanche: 'The Varsouviana'! The polka tune they were playing when Allan—wait!

[*A distant revolver shot is heard. Blanche seems relieved.*]

There now, the shot! It always stops after that.

[*The polka music dies out again.*]

Yes, now it's stopped.

Mitch: Are you boxed out of your mind?"

(*A Streetcar Named Desire*, scene 9, l. 141)

Cinematography has to use codes and conventions and representations that are shared by both film-makers and the audience. The audience constructs meanings in relation to the codes that have meaning in the social world of the movie narration (Bignell 2002: 191). Cinematography uses culturally derived codes, e.g. the mannerisms of the aristocracy as opposed to the proletariat. Codes that cinema shares with other arts, e.g. gestures used in theatre and film. And codes that are unique to cinema. The decoding of signs is an active process, as meaning is constructed by the spectator who is continually adjusting and testing codes. This differs when one is merely reading the meaning from a text (Bignell 2002: 191).

Moreover, film has unique connotative abilities, such as, the film-maker can choose a specific angle, can decide on the camera movements, the colours' intensity, holding longer shots, etc. Most of the times objects are put in a context and that is where the connotative meaning springs from (Monaco 2009: 180). In the scene following the one where Stanley gifts Blanche a return ticket to Laurel on her birthday, we find Blanche sitting on an armchair with her head bent over her body, Stanley and Stella are on their way to the hospital and Blanche is all alone. The shot is taken in such a way that the revolving ceiling fan foregrounds Blanche's crouched figure. The film-maker has angled the camera as such probably in order to draw a sort of parallel between the character and the fan. It could be explained as a kind of motion in fixity.

(Ceiling fan highlighted denoting motion in fixity)

Cinema is a medium of extensions and indices. Much of its meaning comes not from what we don't see (or hear) or, more accurately, from an ongoing process of comparison of what we see with what we don't see (Monaco 2009: 189). *A Streetcar Named Desire* represents gender and culture clash that existed in post-war America in 1947 which was a sharp contrast to the elitist society of Old Southern America. The striking difference is visible in the attitudes of Blanche and Stanley towards life.

> "That's how I'll clear the table! Don't ever talk that way to me! 'Pig—Polack—disgusting—vulgar—greasy!'—them kind of words have been on your tongue and your sister's too much around here! What do you think you two are? A pair of queens? Remember what Huey Long said—'Every Man is a King'. And I am the King around here, so don't forget it!"
>
> (*A Streetcar Named Desire*, scene 8, l. 14)

The said lines are spoken by Stanley Kowalski, who asserts his dominance in the household and makes it quite clear that he won't take kindly to a woman belittling him. Blanche, on the other hand is condescensive and throws her weight around the house since her arrival calling Stanley 'common', 'primitive', 'ape-like', 'brutish', etc. and is audacious enough to say to Stanley:

> But I have been foolish—casting my pearls before...swine. Yes, swine! And I'm thinking not only of you, but of your friend Mr. Mitchell.
>
> (*A Streetcar Named Desire*, scene 10, l. 44)

This subsequently results in the disintegration of Blanche's self-image and sanity. The moment Blanche calls him a 'swine', Stanley loses his amicable mood, rapes her and commits her to an insane asylum in the end. The setting of the play betrays post-war agitation between the sexes. Stanley wants to dominate his home in the same way males-dominated American society before the World War II. The war brought about innumerable changes to the American society. Men from the Allied countries (U.S.A., Britain, France, U.S.S.R., etc.) travelled abroad to fight the Axis nations (Germany, Italy, Japan, Hungary, Romania, Bulgaria) considered as being the greatest enemy of the free world. The women of the Allied countries joined hands and helped in the war effort as the armed forces, service pilots and factory workers both in their home country and abroad. Many of them discovered their independence and tenacity during this time and enjoyed it. However, after the war, most of the men returned to their jobs and the women had to reluctantly return to their roles as homemakers. Thus, female characters like Stella and Blanche expect more than a life of servitude, just as thousands of women after the war wanted to retain their newfound careers and their sense of socio-economic self-worth.

This movie was targeted towards the post-war audience and the censorship uproar did not make any difference to the public which earned the film rave reviews, thus making it a huge box-office success.

WORKS CITED

Barthes, Roland. *Mythologies*. Manchester: Manchester University Press, 1991.

Bignell, Jonathan. *Media Semiotics: An Introduction.* Manchester: Manchester University Press, 2002.

Bluestone, George. *Novels into Films*. Baltimore: John Hopkins University Press, 1957.

Desmond, John M., and Peter Hawkes. *Adaptation: Studying Film and Literature.* Boston: McGraw, 2006.

Dix, Andrew. *Beginning Film Studies*. Manchester: Manchester University Press, 2008.

Hayward, Susan. *Cinema Studies: The Key Concepts.* London: Routhledge, 2000.

Hutcheon, Linda. "Beginning to Theorize Adaptation: What? Who? Why? How? Where? When?", *A Theory of Adaptation.* New York: Routledge, 2006.

Konigsberg, Ira. *The Complete Film Dictionary, Second Edition.* New York: Penguin Putnam Inc., 1998.

Monaco, James. *How to Read a Film: Movies, Media and Beyond: Art, Technology, Language, History, Theory*. Oxford University Press, 2009.

Mulvey, Laura. *Visual and Other Pleasures*. Basingstoke; Macmillan, 1989.

Rowling, J.K. *Harry Potter and the Sorcerer's Stone*. Canada: Scholastic Inc., 2007.

Scholes, Robert et al. *Elements of Literature*. New York: Oxford University Press, 1997.

Williams, Tennessee. *A Streetcar Named Desire*. New York: Penguin, 2009.

ONLINE SOURCES

Susman, G. *This week in Movie History: A Streetcar Named Desire changes screen acting forever*. Retrieved April 1, 2014. www.albany.edu

Technical details of A Streetcar Named Desire. Retrieved April 1, 2014. www.imdb.com

FILM ON DVD

Warner Bros. DVD of Elia Kazan's 1951 *A Streetcar Named Desire.*

Warner Bros. DVD of J.K. Rowling's 2001 *Harry Potter and the Sorcerer's Stone.*

❑❑❑

In Time's Backwater: The Mellowed Sad Glow of a Last Twilight

RAMA KUNDU

I

Island as the Last Vestige of a Receding Past: J.M. Synge's *The Aran Islands*

> In a most desolate stony place[, among]...a passionate and simple race. A correspondence between a lasting mood of the soul and this life that shares the harshness of rocks and winds. (Yeats)

OBVIOUSLY the point of reference is J.M. Synge's *The Aran Islands* (1907). It was Yeats, as it is common knowledge now, who had motivated J.M. Synge, a young dilettante at the time hobnobbing in Paris, towards the Aran Islands on the Atlantic, lying some distance away from the coast of Ireland.

Genesis

To 'express a life that has never found expression'.

Edward J. Obrien writes in his 'Introduction' (1911) to *The Aran Islands*: "the rude but healthy atmosphere of them and of their people had taken possession of a nature ever keen to realise and appropriate new sensations, particularly those which carried with them a deep and noble spiritual import. How magnetic their appeal to the stranger must be was never more fully illustrated than in the intensity of the impression which Mr. Yeats had carried away with him from the islands and communicated to Synge…" (www.sacred-texts.com; to be mentioned henceforth as (*s-t.ai*).

During their meeting in Paris, Yeats had advised Synge to 'give up Paris' (Benson 19): "You will never create anything by reading Racine, and Arthur Symons will always be a better critic of French literature. Go to the Aran islands. Live there as if you were one of the people themselves; express a life that has never found expression" (cited Benson 19) . Till then Synge, a young Irishman, had vaguely thought about being a critic of French literature. Yeats 'communicated' to Synge his own recent experience of the Aran Islands. The impression he made upon Synge was indeed considerable. The advice had its long-term effect, though it took more than one year and a half after this to make his first trip to the Aran. In the meantime he started studying Celtic literature and folklore. Subsequently Synge abandoned his project of 'modern' literary criticism along with its sophisticated tools, and opted instead "for a return to nature as fresh and sincere in its courage and originality as the previous return had been of Coleridge and Wordsworth to the simple standard of truth and beauty" (O'Brien 'Introduction' *s-t.ai*).

# #

Still south I went and west and south again,
Through Wicklow from the morning till the night,
And far from the cities, and the sights of men,
Lived with the sunshine, and the moon's delight.

–Synge, 'Prelude'

Synge set sails, literally, for the Aran Islands in 1898, and then the visit (10 May to 25 June) was repeated four times in the summers of the succeeding years—1899, 1900, 1901, 1902; in all a total of four months and a half was spent on the islands. He settled down on those occasions in the wild desolate place, and adapted himself remarkably to the simple ways of these poor people, still living under the penumbra of a past that had receded from the mainland long ago. It was an isolated strip of land, clinging on to an old fragment of the past from time immemorial, into which the sophisticated youth from Paris took his plunge. "When I look round from the top of these walls I can see the sea on nearly every side, stretching away to distant ranges of mountains on the north and south" (*s-t.ai:* Part I). The visit turned out to be a kind of artistic initiation.

Yeats, in his glowing tribute to Synge in 1910, made two claims for the promising younger artist who had passed away in 1909 at just 38: the claims were about Synge as an artist, and Synge as an Irishman. "He was that rare, that distinguished, that most noble thing", Yeats wrote, "which of all things still of the world is nearest to being sufficient to itself, the pure artist" (Yeats 1961: 323). Secondly, Yeats extolled him for his eager interest in the past of Ireland. "It was...to seek that old Ireland which took its mould from the duellists and scholars of the eighteenth century and from generations older still, that Synge returned again and again to Aran" (Yeats 1961: 324).

Indeed Aran was one of those rare spots where the past, long receded from the mainland, still held on, perhaps because of its geographical seclusion as a cluster of islands, which made the search possible. Simultaneously it was in this secluded wild place that the awakening of the artist in Synge took place.

Synge had visited all the three islands constituting the Aran. Patrick McDonagh's cottage in Inishmann, the middle island, was his favourite resort. But he had also been to Inishmore (north), Inishere (south), the other islands; as he noted nostalgically, "no two journeys to these islands are [/were] alike" (*s-t.ai*; IV). In 1907 the harvest of this experience reached the reader. During these visits he had jotted down his impressions as well as the local anecdotes that had come along his way, in his personal notebooks. Subsequently he revised these into a manuscript, but succeeded to get a publisher only in 1907, by which time his major plays, based on this experience, had already come out. Understandably, the publishers had reasons to be diffident, at least initially, to broach a book about an obscure life in an obscure secluded region little known to the big world outside. Christopher Murray mentions the general resistance to and uneasiness about the book in Ireland long afterwards: "...to the good Catholic population of Ireland Synge was a 'Black Protestant' who could not altogether be trusted as one of our own. Although an excerpt from Synge's *Aran Islands* (1907) was included in the primary-school text *Our National Progress*, in use until the 1960s, it was a safe piece on the difficulties of harvesting and the jolly attitude of the natives rather than anything on the desolation and loneliness of the place or Synge's affinity with its residual pagan beliefs" (Murray 111).

The 'Prelude'

But the importance of the Aran Islands as a document, a literary text, and a 'prelude' to Synge's oeuvre cannot be overestimated. Prior to visiting the Aran Synge was a well-educated man with wide cultural orientation, but not yet a writer. According to Benson, "the Aran Islands were to become Synge's 'objective correlative', furnishing him with both a theme and a style" (Benson 19). According to Yeats, "This life, which he describes elsewhere as the most primitive left in Europe, satisfied some necessity of his nature" (1961: 325). In his inimitable language Yeats elucidates: "it was only when he found Inishmann and the Blaskets, where there is neither riches nor poverty, neither what he calls 'the nullity of the rich' nor 'the squalor of the poor', that his writing lost its old morbid brooding, that he found his genius and his peace" (Yeats 1961: 325). Liammóir writes about Synge's plays: "... he allowed those wild and turbulent people and places to take such possession of his imagination that to see them at their best upon the stage, or to read them in the sober pages of a book, is to pass...into a world so crammed with violence and energy, so melodious with wild splendor, that one feels one has parted the curtains of a quiet lamp-lit room, and seen the lightning leap among the hill-tops at the dawn of day" (vii). The initiation to this splendor had taken place in the Arans.

Yeats recalls his experience of first reading the manuscript of *The Aran Islands*: "I come to understand how much knowledge of the real life of Ireland went to the creation of a world which is yet as fantastic as the Spain of Cervantes" (326). Furthermore, it is this book that eventually turned out to be "the rock upon which Synge's oeuvre is founded". In the words of Robin Skelton: "*The Aran Islands* is, like Yeats' *The Celtic Twilight*, not merely an attempt to report upon the persistence of ancient culture and beliefs among the Irish peasantry, but a construction of images and values which have validity in themselves.... If *The Aran Islands* is the rock upon which Synge's oeuvre is founded, it is not the rock of newly recovered fact but that of fact transformed by the imagination into a vision of universal significance and creative utility" (40). Here we have a picture of a real island, which is yet endowed in the narrator's perception with the charm and spell of a dream-isle.

The Aran Island (1907) of J.M. Synge (1871-1909), famed as Ireland's own island-writer, is about a real cluster of islands, yet it seems to belong indeed to the domain of a 'fantastic' dream, a rare wonderful fragment of life floated down from the past; an archway, as it were, for the artistic mind to reach the primitive solitude of the earth and the sky, beyond the mundane success/failures of modern life. It is a picture of the remote islands in the lap of nature, and their marginalised residents carrying on an ancient lifestyle,—perceived by the artist's eye, and painted lovingly with tender simple brush-strokes.

On the first day of disembarking Synge had felt he had never seen a more desolate scene. Rugged hills crawled up from the sea to disappear behind fog. Under incessant rain streams of grey water spread everywhere upon the slate-coloured stone; the only path had turned a raging stream that encircled the low hills, sped through the small farmlands and bushes, touching along its passage some desolate church or school building, some stone-pillars with the cross on top. Amidst this backdrop there survived a few islanders leading the life of abject poverty.

Yet, Synge had felt that this life, lived to the never-ceasing chant of the sea, was like some ancient poetry or folklore. The people and the creatures that lived around—building nests, or burrowing into the earth—had the same proximity to nature, nearly the same naturalness. Most of the equipments were handmade from natural material. *Curgah*, the slim rowing boat, ran across the water like some pony, hoisting its small sail; perhaps the first sea-voyagers, Synge conjectures, had sailed out precisely by similar boats. Men walked like some wild animal, with similar pace, straightness, simple dignity. They spoke as if from within some dream, to the rhythm of the waves. With these properties of wild creatures met the taste and grace of some ancient society. And there was the deep tender familial bond. Yearlong they lived in the grey world of rain and fog; so the children and girls nestling in the little warm corner of the kitchen took such a unique place in their consciousness, which the modern society outside won't be able to grasp.

Towards the brink of the sea where fog and foam play with fingers intertwined, there among the seaweeds girls stand, busy at their work—looking like some sea-bird with their white legs skirted by red petticoats; while their faces bear a queer 'spiritual expression'. An old man tells stories about fairies, tells about girls supposedly taken away by the fairies. While listening to these tales Synge feels that the extraordinary, 'unearthly' beauty of the girls may have some mysterious connection with these tales. The fairies have also taken some men. One such is claimed to have been seen to ride about on a white horse in the morning and evening twilights. They are even supposed to cause shipwrecks. The old man is sure one of his children has been stolen by the fairies.

During rain, churning black water makes its way everywhere; the wind shrieks and whistles as it rages along. On such days the bottle of *poteen* comes out from its hiding—it is also of the same grey colour as the sky and the sea—to make the evening bearable. When death strikes, the funeral party is also sustained by the same *poteen*.

The grieving women 'keen' on the rocky beach—breaking down upon the shingles like the sea-waves that break down on the rough shore and burst into foam. This articulate grief of a people, who are usually silent, suddenly exposes a concealed heart—the heart that has been rent by helpless desolation, worn away by the endless struggle with the storm and the sea. Then the thunder explodes like the last gun-salute of the island to death, the rumbling drowning all other sounds.

This Aran shall be found no more in the tourists' spot of today. Yet it has remained immortal in the writings of Synge as a land of exquisite beauty and solitude, of fairies and the ancient lores.

Genre

...these unarranged, unspeculative pages. (Yeats)

How to define the genre of *The Aran Islands*?

Synge said, "I look on *The Aran Islands* as my first serious piece of work" (*Prose* 47; cited Benson 18). In his 'Author's Foreword' Synge says, "In the pages that follow I have given a direct account of my life on the islands, and of what I met with among them, inventing nothing, and changing nothing that is essential". The element of authenticity is apparent. He admits of course, "As far as possible, however, I have disguised the identity of the people I speak of, by making changes in their names, and in the letters I quote, and by altering some local and family relationships. I have had nothing to say about them that was not wholly in their favour, but I have made this disguise to keep them from ever feeling that a too direct use had been made of their kindness, and friendship, for which I am more grateful than it is easy to say." The gesture reflects the same cordiality, friendliness, and dignified modesty that remain Synge's hallmark in these pages.

Benson compares the book to Wordsworth's *The Prelude* on certain points: firstly, Wordsworth's principle as enunciated in the Preface to the second edition of *Lyrical Ballads*, that in the humble and rustic ways of life human passions were at one with the beautiful forms of nature. Synge was quite clear in his mind about the purpose of the book, that it was going to be neither a guide book nor a travelogue, offering useful information of the present and past of the place. It was rather the intimate talk of a diarist with himself, and in course of the process unfolding his mind at an important turn of his artistic growth. In Benson's words: here the author "reveals primarily the manner in which the Aran Islands shaped his artistic sensibility and only secondarily the lives and customs of the island people. *The Aran Island* is as autobiographical as *The Prelude* and might well have been subtitled 'Growth of a Dramatist's Mind'" (Benson 25).

The narrator as an outsider is registering his fresh personal impressions and responses through a fragmented narrative. Yet it is not his self-portrait; it is rather the impressionistic portrait of an ancient place with its mysterious beauty and spell. In *The Aran Islands* Synge told not only of the sea, the birds, the storms, but also about the simple people, and the charming beauty of their hard life and simple primitive ways. He had also learnt the Gaelic language, mastered its idiom, as the book bears its evidence.

Yeats underscores the simple clarity and spontaneity between the lines of "these unarranged, unspeculative pages". Indeed it is in these pages, his first book, though published later, that Synge can be found at his best in some respects. In the words of Yeats: "He was no nearer when we walked and talked than now while I read these unarranged, unspeculative pages, wherein the only life he loved with his whole heart reflects itself as in the still water of a pool. Thought comes to him slowly, and only after long, seemingly unmeditative watching, and when it comes...it is spoken without hesitation and never changed" (1961:328). In this essay Yeats gives a clue to Synge's way of responding to the Aran islands.

The Aran Islands is a fragmentary narrative in the first-person, in the journal form, made out in four parts; showing aesthetic sensitivity as well as receptivity towards the extraordinary, the intense, the wild nature. In the book, we find an arrivant from the outside world observing the island, surprised, absorbed, enraptured; sometimes "sitting over a turf fire" like the indwellers, and learning ballads which would soon be on their way out, listening to the strange tales woven round their strange simple life. Synge's plays are better known than this book. But here, in these strange yet real-life stories/anecdotes lie the seeds of his masterpieces,—*Riders to the Sea*, *In the Shadow of the Glen*, *The Playboy*, etc.

He noted with awe the desolation, the solitude and the peace of the natural scenario, and the rippling vitality of humans side by side; the pagan beliefs and attitudes lingering beside the recent Christian ones; the primitive life and the cultured ways going hand in hand in a very special manner; while the mystery of the supernatural got twined with the despair of mortality.

The [Is]Landscape

I have seen nothing so desolate....

Synge recounts his first glimpse of the Arans in terms of dreariness: "A dreary rock appeared at first sloping up from the sea into the fog" (*s-t. ai*; I). He records his first experience of rain upon the island.

> I have seen nothing so desolate. Grey floods of water were sweeping everywhere upon the limestone, making at times a wild torrent of the road, which twined continually over low hills and cavities in the rock or passed between a few small fields of potatoes or grass hidden away in corners that had shelter. Whenever the cloud lifted I could see the edge of the sea below me on the right, and the naked ridge of the island above me on the other side. Occasionally I passed a lonely chapel or schoolhouse, or a line of stone pillars with crosses above them and inscriptions asking a prayer for the soul of the person they commemorated. (*s-t.ai*; I)

On the day of leaving the middle island, again he feels:

> The island had never seemed so desolate. Looking out over the black limestone through the driving rain to the gulf of struggling waves, an indescribable feeling of dejection came over me (*s-t.ai*; II). On his second visit he writes: "This year I see a darker side of life in the islands. The sun seldom shines, and day after day a cold south-western wind blows over the cliffs, bringing up showers of hail and dense masses of cloud. (*s-t.ai*; II)

Sometimes it can be as desolate as anything, and thereby stirring the same mood in the narrator.

> A week of sweeping fogs has passed over and given me a strange sense of exile and desolation. I walk round the island nearly every day, yet I can see nothing anywhere but a mass of wet rock, a strip of surf, and then a tumult of waves.
>
> The slaty limestone has grown black with the water that is dripping on it, and wherever I turn there is. The same grey obsession twining and wreathing itself among the narrow fields, and the same wail from the wind that shrieks and whistles in the loose rubble of the walls.
>
> At first the people do not give much attention to the wilderness that is round them, but after a few days their voices sink in the kitchen, and their endless talk of pigs and cattle falls to the whisper of men who are telling stories in a haunted house.
>
> The rain continues (*s-t.ai*; I)

Yet, he enjoyed the place. An endless expanse of grey water, and in its midst tiny dots of grey rocky islands, hazy under the overhanging mist and fog—these are the Aran islands on the Atlantic south of the Irish coast. The people there too seem to get merged into these wild sandy dunes, the froth/foam thrown up by the tossing waves, the roaring wind, the ceaseless rumbling of the sea breaking upon the shore; they too are, as it were, partly nature's own. Hard, unstable, insecure life under the perpetual shadow of death, a little farming, fishing, netting, running the family; in the evening story-telling sessions around the flickering light from handmade lamps or fire of dry grass, where 'fairies' are allowed to step in without hindrance or inhibition.

People

> The charm which the people over there (Inishmaan) share with the birds and flowers. (s-t.ai; III)
>
> I would have liked to turn the prow to the west and row with them for ever.

Synge writes during his second visit: "I am in the north island again, looking out with a singular sensation to the cliffs across the sound. It is hard to believe that those hovels I can just see in the south are filled with people whose lives have the strange quality that is found in the oldest poetry and legend" (*s-t.ai*; II).

Yeats found the people and life here as something particularly congenial for Synge's temperament; he observed: "Here were men and women who under the weight of their necessity lived, as the artist lives, in the presence of death and childhood, and the great affections and the orgiastic moment when life outleaps its limits, and who, as it is always with those who have refused or escaped the trivial and the temporary, had dignity and good manners where manners mattered" (Yeats 1961: 325).

Indeed, this book shows how authentic are the life and language depicted in his plays, even to minute detail. Synge saw how every aspect of their simple, dignified life was conditioned by the sea, the wind, the encircled island.

The narrator is charmed by the simplicity of the humble dwellers; by their clinging attachment to the family: "For these people the outrage to the hearth is the supreme catastrophe. They live here in a world of grey, where there are wild rains and mists every week in the year, and their warm chimney corners, filled with children and young girls, grow into the consciousness of each family in a way it is not easy to understand in more civilised places" (*s-t.ai*; I).

People: Primitivism

> These strange men with receding foreheads, high cheekbones, and ungovernable eyes seem to represent some old type found on these few acres at the extreme border of Europe, where it is only.... (*s-t.ai*; III)

While referring to the element of primitivism in *The Aran Islands*, Benson is reminded of another artist, Gauguin, who had left Paris and sailed off to a remote island in search of prmitivism. However, for Synge this primitivism is associated with perfection which he admires and does not look down upon, never. Even the absence of the heavy boots of Europe appears to have given them "the agile walk of the wild animal, while the general simplicity of their lives has given them many other points of physical perfection" (*s-t.ai*; I). The primitive aspect of the island enraptured him: "the life is perhaps most primitive that is left in Europe".

He had reached out to this people with an authenticity of feeling that rises above all sentimentality. He did not seek to idealise them in spite of his attraction and occasional rapture; he just saw them as they were, and loved them as such.

Simplicity

The author is charmed by the naturalness of their ways of life, and particularly by the unique simplicity: "these men of Inishmaan seemed to be moved by strange archaic sympathies with the world. Their mood accorded itself with wonderful fineness to the suggestions of the day, and their ancient Gaelic seemed so full of divine simplicity that *I would have liked to turn the prow to the west and row with them for ever*" (*s-t.ai;* III; emphasis added).

He looks fascinated even at the simple small articles created by the local people, their antique beauty, and naturalness.

"Every article on these islands has an almost personal character, which gives this simple life, where all art is unknown, something of the artistic beauty of medieval life. The curaghs and spinning-wheels, the tiny wooden barrels that are still much used in the place of earthenware, the home-made cradles, churns, and baskets, are all full of individuality, and being made from materials that are common here, yet to some extent peculiar to the island, they seem to exist as a natural link between the people and the world that is about them" (*s-t.ai;* I).

Even such small details as the footwear and its connection with their walking/dancing gait are noted attentively.

"The absence of the heavy boot of Europe has preserved to these people the agile walk of the wild animal, while the general simplicity of their lives has given them many other points of physical perfection. Their way of life has never been acted on by anything much more artificial than the nests and burrows of the creatures that live round them, and they seem, in a certain sense, to approach more nearly to the finer types of our aristocracies—who are bred artificially to a natural ideal—than to the labourer or citizen, as the wild horse resembles the thoroughbred rather than the hack or cart-horse. Tribes of the same natural development are, perhaps, frequent in half-civilized countries, but here a touch of the refinement of old societies is blended, with singular effect, among the qualities of the wild animal" (*s-t.ai*; I).

He notes the beauty of the simple dress-up with the aesthetician's eye. "The simplicity and unity of the dress increases in another way the local air of beauty. The women wear red petticoats and jackets of the island wool stained with madder, to which they usually add a plaid shawl twisted around their chests and tied at the back. When it rains they throw another petticoat over their heads with the waistband around their faces, or, if they are young, they use a heavy shawl like those worn in Galway" (*s-t.ai*; I).

He learns from them respect for the sea; "as the old man gave me his view of the use of fear.

'A man who is not afraid of the sea will soon be drowned,' he said, 'for he will be going out on a day he shouldn't. But we do be afraid of the sea, and we do only be drownded now and again'" (*s-t.ai*; II).

Their secluded island-life has made them master of all trades, including netting, fishing, rope-making; rye and potato-growing; animal-keeping; each a skilled fisherman, an expert sailor, farmer, kelp-burner, shoe-maker, net-mender, builder, thatcher, cradle-maker, coffin-maker, according to the seasons and needs. So intensely alive that work never becomes dull for him. Synge finds: "It is likely that much of the intelligence and charm of these people is due to the absence of any division of labour, and to the correspondingly wide development of each individual, whose varied knowledge and skill necessitates a considerable activity of mind" (*s-t.ai*; III).

People: Artists

Watching a number of red and grey figures hurrying about their work on the low sheets of rock to the east, he feels: "The continual passing in this island between the misery of last night and the splendor of to-day, seems to create an affinity between the moods of these people and the moods of varying rapture and dismay that are frequent in artists, and in certain forms of alienation. Yet it is only in the intonation of a few sentences or some old fragment of melody that I catch the real spirit of the island (*s-t.ai*; I).

Elsewhere he observes,—"The danger of his life on the sea gives him [the islander] the alertness of the primitive hunter, and the long nights he spends fishing in his curagh bring him some of the emotion that are thought peculiar to men who have lived with the arts" (*s-t.ai*; III).

The Music

The island and its people have their own music to which Synge listens enraptured.

"Underneath me to the east there is the one inhabited district of the island, where I can see red figures moving about the cottages, sending up an occasional fragment of conversation or of old island melodies."

Synge describes a musical evening in which he had listened to a youth and an old woman; "several times when the young man finished a poem she took it up again and recited the verses with exquisite musical intonation, putting a wistfulness and passion into her voice that seemed to give it all the cadences that are sought in the profoundest poetry.

The lamp had burned low, and another terrible gale was howling and shrieking over the island. It seemed like a dream that I should be sitting here among these men and women listening to this rude and beautiful poetry that is filled with the oldest passions of the world" (*s-t.ai*; II).

Keening

> This grief of the keen...seems to contain the whole passionate rage ...in every native of the island.

Keening is also a kind of collective music sung in chorus. Synge had often listened in awe to this music of the Aran.

"While the grave was being opened the women sat down among the flat tombstones, bordered with a pale fringe of early bracken, and began the wild keen, or crying for the dead. Each old woman, as she took her turn in the leading recitative, seemed possessed for the moment with a profound ecstasy of grief, swaying to and fro, and bending her forehead to the stone before her, while she called out to the dead with a perpetually recurring chant of sobs.

All round the graveyard other wrinkled women, looking out from under the deep red petticoats that cloaked them, rocked themselves with the same rhythm, and intoned the inarticulate chant that is sustained by all as an accompaniment" (*s-t.ai*; I).

The morning had been beautifully fine, but as they lowered the coffin into the grave, thunder rumbled overhead and hailstones hissed among the bracken. This incidental trifle would prompt Synge to read an empathy between man and nature in this island.

> In Inishmaan one is forced to believe in *a sympathy between man and nature*, and at this moment when the thunder sounded a death-peal of extraordinary grandeur above the voices of the women, I could see the faces near me stiff and drawn with emotion.
>
> When the coffin was in the grave, and the thunder had rolled away across the hills of Clare, the keen broke out again more passionately than before.
>
> *This grief of the keen is no personal complaint for the death of one woman over eighty years, but seems to contain the whole passionate rage that lurks somewhere in every native of the island.* In this cry of pain the inner consciousness of the people seems to lay itself bare for an instant, and to reveal the mood of beings who feel their isolation in the face of a universe that wars on them with winds and seas. They are usually silent, but in the presence of death all outward show of indifference or patience is forgotten, and they shriek with pitiable despair before the horror of the fate to which they are all doomed. (*s-t.ai*; I; emphasis added)

Doomed

> I knew that every one of them would be drowned in the sea in a few years and battered naked on the rocks.

The author does not highlight the religious ritualistic features of a burial; instead he perceives it in the light of elementality. Benson comments: "The sea in both *The Aran Islands* and *Riders to the Sea* is a complex symbol of mortality and the point made by Synge in both works is that all men and women are riders destined to be drowned in that sea"

(Benson 29). Synge has described scenes of burial by the sea, under the rocks, to the music of high wind, and service of tossing waves, blinding lightning, and deafening thunder.

> As they talked to me and gave me a little poteen and a little bread when they thought I was hungry, I could not help feeling that I was talking with men who were under a judgment of death. I knew that every one of them would be drowned in the sea in a few years and battered naked on the rocks, or would die in his own cottage and be buried with another fearful scene in the graveyard I had come from. (*s-t.ai*; IV)

He is also drawn strongly by scenes of risen nature and human calamity including disaster and death; for instance by a scene of burial with thunder rumbling overhead, and hailstones hissing among the bracken.

It is the vision of a world of doomed men, pitted against a wild nature. The island scenario helps to further accentuate this sense of doom and mystery and the intensity of it all. Valour, grief, exultation, despondency all get accommodated in this vision. Hence Synge's pictures of sailing, fishing, drawn in bold strokes bring out the immense challenge of this life and the heroic acceptance of the same. Incidentally, Synge, whose life was to be cut short at just thirty-eight, was himself haunted by a sense of doom,

> They'll say I came in Eighteen-seventy-one,
> And died in Dublin.... What year will they write
> For my poor passage to the stall of night?
>
> ("On an Anniversary" in Synge 1972; 229)

In 1908, he wrote the poem "I've Thirty Months", which proved true before long.

Doom and Women

The women, he found, were doomed in a very pathetic way, left often lonely, helpless, bereaved, and eventually destroyed; with no choice but to take the battering as it comes.

"The maternal feeling is so powerful on these islands that it gives a life of torment to the women. Their sons grow up to be banished as soon as they are of age, or to live here in continual danger on the sea; their daughters go away also, or are worn out in their youth with bearing children that grow up to harass them in their own turn a little later" (*s-t.ai*; II). The beauty and the pathos of the island life are, the narrator finds, accentuated in the women's features and life,—beautiful, pathetic, warm-hearted and long-suffering as they are.

Doom and Carnival

...to keep sanity in men who live forgotten in these worlds of mist.

Carnival and death are locked in embrace in this doomed life bounded by the sea and patterned by stark nature:

> There is quaint humour, and sometimes wild humour, on the middle island, but never this half-sensual ecstasy of laughter. Perhaps a man must have a sense of intimate misery,...before he can set himself to jeer and mock at the world. (*s-t.ai*; III)

Exhilaration and despondency are the two strings upon which the Arans play its music.

> The lightness of the pampooties seems to make the dancing on this island lighter and swifter than anything I have seen on the mainland, and the simplicity of the men enables them to throw a naïve extravagance into their steps that is impossible in places where the people are self-conscious (*s-t.ai*; IV).

When the rain continues day after day, at such a turn a hidden aspect comes to light: "but this evening a number of young men were in the kitchen mending nets, and the bottle of poteen was drawn from its hiding-place./ One cannot think of these people drinking wine on the summit of this crumbling precipice, but their grey poteen, which brings a shock of joy to the blood, seems predestined to keep sanity in men who live forgotten in these worlds of mist" (*s-t.ai*; I). This is the carnival of "these people who are wearied of the sea" (*s-t.ai*; II), who are haunted by a sense of doom.

During times of continued rain they have recourse to their own merriment: "I sat in the kitchen part of the evening to feel the gaiety that was rising, and when I came into my own room after dark, one of the sons came in every time the bottle made its round, to pour me out my share" (*s-t.ai*; I).

> When we had all come out of the graveyard, and two men had rebuilt the hole in the wall through which the coffin had been carried in, we walked back to the village, talking of anything, and joking of anything, as if merely coming from the boat-slip, or the pier. (*s-t.ai*; I)

One of them tells Synge of the poteen drinking that takes place at some funerals.

> "A while since," he said, "there were two men fell down in the graveyard while the drink was on them. The sea was rough that day, the way no one could go to bring the doctor, and one of the men never woke again, and found death that night." (*s-t.ai*; I)

Law

> They took the gallows from the slack,/ They set it on the glen,/ They hang'd the proud Sheriff on that,/ And released their own three men—
>
> —'Robin Hood and the Widow's Three Sons'
>
> (*Oxford Book of Ballads* 621)

It is part of the people's carnival all over the world to disregard 'Law'. The narrator understands, sensitively and sympathetically, the islanders' non-conformist approach to law, which is similar to that revealed in the *Robinhood ballads*,[1] in the *Wessex Tales* of Hardy ("The Three Strangers", "The Distracted Preacher", for example). From his close experience of the norms and ethos of the Aran society Synge had come to realise:

> It seems absurd to apply the same laws to these people and to the criminal classes of a city. The most intelligent man on Inishmaan has often spoken to me of his contempt of the law, and of the increase of crime the police have brought to Aranmor. On this island, he says, if men have a little difference, or a little fight, their friends take care it does not go too far, and in a little time it is forgotten. (*s-t.ai*)

Exhilaration: Exultation

> this death, with the fresh sea saltness in one's teeth, would be better than most deaths one is likely to meet.

Apart from the carnival of the local folk, we encounter on occasions another kind of exhilaration in these pages, which is the author's own. For instance, while getting from one island to another,

> the motion became strangely exhilarating. Even, I thought, if we were dropped into the blue chasm of the waves, this death, with the fresh sea saltness in one's teeth, would be better than most deaths one is likely to meet. (*s-t.ai*; I)

On another occasion, with waves coming up upon waves, "the excitement was too great to allow time for fear" (*s-t.ai*; II). While wandering on the cliffs during a storm:

> Immense masses of spray were flying up from the base of the cliff, …I had to crouch down for an instant, wrapped and blinded by a white hail of foam. (*s-t.ai*; II)

"The waves were so enormous that when I saw one more than usually large coming towards me, I turned instinctively to hide myself, as one blinks when struck upon the eyes" (*s-t.ai*; II). But perhaps this was too much for the human mind to take for long.

> After a few hours the mind grows bewildered with the endless change and struggle of the sea, and an utter despondency replaces the first moment of exhilaration. (*s-t.ai*; II)

Supernatural

> These people make no distinction between the natural and the supernatural. (*s-t.ai*; III)

The islands are observed and depicted as a domain of mystery where broad outlines are made to disappear behind mist/fog. This reality verges on the surreality. Synge is struck by "The supernatural beauty that comes over the island so often in rainy weather" (*s-t.ai*; I). The island and islanders equally accommodate stark reality and the mysterious supernatural within its ambience.

Wonder was an accepted element in the islanders' life. "On these islands alone miracles enough happen every year to equip a divine emissary Rye is turned into oats, storms are raised to keep evictors from the shore, cows that are isolated on lonely rocks bring forth calves, and other things of the same kind are common.

The wonder is a rare expected event, like the thunderstorm or the rainbow, except that it is a little rarer and a little more wonderful."

Synge registers some of his strange dreams which are also in tune with the rest of the place; he frankly admits:

"Some dreams I have had in this cottage seem to give strength to the opinion that there is a psychic memory attached to certain neighbourhoods.

"In a moment I was swept away in a whirlwind of notes. My breath and my thoughts and every impulse of my body, became a form of the dance,... For a while it seemed an excitement that was filled with joy, then it grew into an ecstasy where all existence was lost in a vortex of movement.... At last with a moment of uncontrollable frenzy I broke back to consciousness and awoke.

> .... The moon was glittering across the bay, and there was no sound anywhere on the island. (*s-t.ai*; I)

Synge made effective use of local superstitions in his plays; for instance Maurya in *Riders to the Sea* sees dead Michael on horseback and knows Bartley will die, because the dead need companionship. In Murray's words: "Maurya's knowledge comes from beyond the grave.... So strong is Synge's empathy with the kind of people he met and lived among on Aran that superstition is not a factor in the play. These people live so close to death that it is always round the next corner" (Murray 116).

The Lonely Man among Doomed Men and Women

Solitude:

> He was a drifting silent man full of hidden passion, and loved wild islands, because there, set out in the light of day, he saw what lay hidden in himself. (Yeats)

Liammóir writes in his 'Introduction' to Synge's selected works: "He shook people to their foundations by the sheer reality of his mind, by the strange unrealistic reality of his ear and of his method, by the relentless rich reality of his solitude" (Liammóir v-vi).

Watching *curaghs* landing at the slip through heavy roll, roaming in the dark nights, wandering on the stormy days, he had the salt on his body and tongue.

"I have been down sitting on the pier till it was quite dark. I am only beginning to understand the nights of Inishmaan and the influence they have had in giving distinction to these men who do most of their work after nightfall.

I could hear nothing but a few curlews and other wild-fowl whistling and shrieking in the seaweed, and the low rustling of the waves. It was one of the dark sultry nights peculiar to September, with no light anywhere except the phosphorescence of the sea, and an occasional rift in the clouds that showed the stars behind them.

The sense of solitude was immense. I could not see or realise my own body, and I seemed to exist merely in my perception of the waves and of the crying birds, and of the smell of seaweed" (*s-t.ai*; III). It is the artist's personal response to the abounding solitude.

Synge used to take part in their revelry, of course in his quiet way; sometimes fiddling inside the cottage during such an event." After the dancing and excitement we were too stirred up to be sleepy, so we sat for a long time round the embers of the turf, talking and smoking by the light of the candle" (Part IV). In the same way he quietly participated in their grieving.

> I went out again to look over the sea, but night had fallen and the hurricane was howling over the Dun. I walked down the lane and heard the keening in the house where the young man was. Further on I could see a stir about the door of the cottage that had been last struck by typhus. Then I turned back again in the teeth of the rain, and sat over the fire with the old man and woman talking of the sorrows of the people till it was late in the night. (*s-t.ai*; IV)

The artist's enjoyment is shown in the fine accuracy of description of the revelry of nature:

> As I lie here hour after hour, I seem to enter into the wild pastimes of the cliff, and to become a companion of the cormorants and crows. Many of the birds display themselves before me with the vanity of barbarians, performing in strange evolutions as long as I am in sight, and returning to their ledge of rock when I am gone. Some are wonderfully expert, and cut graceful figures for an inconceivable time without a flap of their wings, growing so absorbed in their own dexterity that they often collide with one another in their flight, an incident always followed by a wild outburst of abuse. Their language is easier than Gaelic, and I seem to understand the greater part of their cries, though I am not able to answer. There is one plaintive note which they take up in the middle of their usual babble with extraordinary effect, and pass on from one to another along the cliff with a sort of an inarticulate wail, as if they remembered for an instant the horror of the mist. (*s-t.ai*)

The primitive life and the starkness of nature in the isles had stirred some deep chord within. Usually a man of reserve and control, in Aran he has often been stirred to an intensity of feeling,—"almost to the pitch of a neurotic hyperaesthesis" (M. Bourgeois, *John M. Synge and the Irish Theatre*, NY: Blom, 1965, p. 92). Benson comments on the language and imagery of *The Aran Islands* as "charged and intensely emotional". Examples abound: for instance his response to the storm, which leaves the "bay full of green delirium".

He had keenly intensely enjoyed the island, its air-water-sky-wind-rocks-sand, and communicates some of his keen feelings to the reader;

perhaps that is why these 'unregulated, unspeculative' notes can retain their charm even today.

Not that the Aran made him; rather he found it particularly congenial to his make-up; as he wrote in one of his last poems, "Prelude":

> I knew the stars, the flowers, and the birds,
> The grey and wintry sides of many glens,
> And did but half remember human words,
> In converse with the mountains, moors, and fens (Synge 1954; 232)

> ...for...he was one of those for whom the important things served as a prelude to that wild and lonely mood in earth and sky that lies beyond the success or failure of the lives of men. (Liammóir x)

The Yearning for a Unique but Receding Past

> The sort of yearning I feel towards those lonely rocks is indescribably acute.

Towards the end of Part I, the author looks back to the Islands with a yearning love, and compares them to the mainland: "to stroll along the edge of Galway bay, and look out in the direction of the islands. The sort of yearning I feel towards those lonely rocks is indescribably acute. This town, that is usually so full of wild human interest, seems in my present mood a tawdry medley of all that is crudest in modern life. The nullity of the rich and the squalor of the poor give me the same pang of wondering disgust; yet the islands are fading already and I can hardly realise that the smell of the seaweed and the drone of the Atlantic are still moving round them" (*s-t.ai*; I).

Indeed Synge's book stirs a nostalgia in the reader's mind as well, even those readers who are born in another part of the globe, for a beautiful lost world.

By crossing the boundary/barrier of the mundane and arriving at the domain of the extraordinary, here he found 'the spiritual treasure', 'the magnet' of his soul, 'every symbol of the cosmos in its timeless images' of nature and life. The result is this dreamy yet passionate viewing of a unique beauty, constituted by the peace and dignity of nature and people. During his last visit Synge writes:

> as I waited, with just light enough from the chimney to let me see the rafters and the greyness of the walls, I became indescribably mournful, for I felt that this little corner on the face of the world,

> and the people who live in it, have a peace and dignity from which we are shut for ever. (*s-t.ai*; IV)

While claiming that "Synge came close to creating an age in Ireland: ...he more than any other showed Ireland to the world", Liammóir takes care to points out "it was an Ireland neither of fact nor of fiction but of a creative revelation" (Liammóir x). And the process started with *The Aran Islands*.

Christopher Murray accepts the suggestion that a "tragic vision unifies Synge's work" as a legitimate and challenging way of looking at his plays (115); "*Riders*, for all its brevity...has in its foreboding and inevitability the air of Greek tragedy.... The world it (*Riders*) conjures up is remote, ancient, primitive in the positive cultural sense. It dramatizes the struggle for survival in its most Darwinian and elemental form. It denies the consolations of religious belief" (Murray 115-16). This is the world we find in *The Aran Islands*. It is indeed *The Aran Islands* that can be read between the lines of *Riders* and his other plays.

Synge had claimed: "*The Aran Islands* throws a good deal of light on my plays" (Foreword). In addition to illuminating the origin of plot, and image, and word-play *The Aran Islands* continues to hold the keys to his later work. "It is the value-system created in this book that gives us an indication of the attitude we must have in reading the later drama" (Skelton 39).

Synge's own time and country failed to take into account the stark tragic note and the picture of untarnished life in *The Aran Islands*. But a most eminent Irish artist had noted in "these unarranged, unspeculative pages" "a correspondence between a lasting mood of the soul and this life that shares the harshness of rocks and winds". Yeats conjectures about the secret of this strange island's appeal to Synge: "He loves all that has edge, all that is salt in the mouth, all that is rough to the hand, all that heightens the emotions by contest, all that stings into life the sense of tragedy; and in this book, unlike the plays where nearness to his audience moves him to mischief, he shows it without thought of other taste than his. It is so constant, it is set out so simply, so naturally, that it suggests a correspondence between a lasting mood of the soul and this life that shares the harshness of rocks and winds" (1961: 326-27).

Benson argues: "The importance of Synge's experiences on the Aran Islands cannot be overestimated; here he found the plots of three of his plays, and innumerable incidents, images, and turns of speech that provided the raw data on which his creative imagination could work" (Benson 32). But it was much more than that; it involved a spiritual journey and the growth of an artist's soul.

Yeats' beautiful simple lines perhaps offer a most appropriate summing up of Synge's brief but intense passage through the Arans and through life.

> long travelling, he had come
> Towards nightfall among certain set apart
> In a most desolate stony place,
> Towards nightfall upon a race
> Passionate and simple like his heart.
> (Yeats, "In Memory of Major Robert Gregory", *Collected Poems*, 2008: 108)

II

A Doomed Man among a Doomed People

Margaret Craven: *I Heard the Owl Call My Name* (1967)

> Come swimmer ...
> The village is you....

An island usually implies an is[olated]land; and because of this circumstantial factor, a remote island—geographically far-flung, and difficult of access—can sometimes turn out to be a unique backwater of 'Time', by retaining the characteristic features-ways-attitudes of a chunk of the old times, which have long disappeared from the mainland metropolis. This clinging to the remnants of an old forgotten past (also already in the process of waning) lends a particular pathetic charm, like the mellowed sad glow of a last twilight, upon the place and people inhabiting there. It is this mellowed perception of an island as the last vestige of a receding past that we find in J.M. Synge's *The Aran Islands*, and Margaret Craven's *I Heard the Owl Call My Name*.

The nuances and attraction of such an actual island off the coast of Ireland had been captured by J.M. Synge in 1907; and sixty years after Synge another such island at one of the furthest points of Canada was evoked by Margaret Craven, leaving two unique island texts for posterity.

In *I Heard the Owl Call My Name* (1967), Margaret Craven (1901-80) evokes a remote island-space, caught up in a backwater of time, and fragrant with memory of and nostalgia for an even older time which has started receding from it. She presents a unique picture of an isolated space which provides an appropriate backdrop for the penultimate pursuit of a simple devout mind.

In many ways it is not only different but nearly contrapuntal to Synge's book, written six decades ago, on another beautiful obscure island, also left alone in time's backwater. Yet, the points of comparison too are many and worth consideration. In both the books we have an outsider looking in awe and admiration at the inside. Synge writes in the first person about his own perceptions and impressions, whereas the impressions and experiences of Craven's protagonist have been reported by the omniscient author. But whereas Synge had been just the 'noble man from the mainland', Mark, the young vicar, who is initially more of an outsider among the indigenous native Canadians, as he hails from the colonizing race, the "white man", eventually finds his last 'home' there.

I Heard the Owl ... (to be mentioned hereafter as *IHO*) is a fiction though based on factual account of a place, and people, including the outsider who turned insider in course of the story. The story, whatever little of it is there, is told in the manner of a fragmented narration, as one may encounter in a journal-entry or diary. Though told in the omniscient author's voice, it is primarily the young outsider's point of view from which we see the place, the people, and the sparse happenings, except the end, when the viewer/respondent has already passed away.

It is about the last one year and a few months in the life of Mark Brian, a young vicar, which are spent on an island, and dedicated to serve the people of this place in the backwaters of non-white 'original' Canada,—cut off from the big outside world by countless tortuous inlets, icy sea and rivers, sharp wind, dangerous mountains and forests. It is again a place in which the last remnants of an ancient society and culture still linger on in its last twilight, though the process of extinction of the old ways has already started. In its vulnerable in-between situation the island seems to offer a parallel/analogy to the terminally ill young vicar; both being on their way out. Craven's charming narrative captures both the courses in the glow of a sad, brief, exquisite twilight.

It is a real island space on which an imaginary fiction of slender but graceful outlines has been hoisted. The author had learnt about the place first from her twin brother Wilson, who had been there, and subsequently from studying accounts of the indigenous culture; later, in 1962, she herself visited Kingcome by arrangement with the Columbia Coast Mission of the Anglican Church. In this book Craven sensitively and fondly recaptures the remote isle and its adjacent inlets, the hard life of its sparsely populated villages still retaining an old fragment of a time, which is getting eroded bit by bit with every passing year. The narration seems to throb and quiver with a fine nostalgia. It is not an intense reaction, but it is a deep tenderness that she brings to treat her subject constituted by the nature and the inhabitants of the small island-village.

"Kwakiutl" is the name of the tribe whose home is this Kingcome, this farthest island-village in British Columbia of Canada. The bishop, on coming to know of the illness of his young vicar, sends him to this place, the "hardest parish" (*IHO* 3) under his jurisdiction, so that the best in him is drawn out and "buckled" (*à la* Hopkins, "The Windhover") here. The spot is hard to reach; in answer to the polite question of a local hostess, 'how did you like our river?', a previous bishop had said drily "that getting into heaven could be no harder than reaching this village, and...was bound to be warmer" (*IHO* 24). Like the actual island, it is indeed icy, remote, necessitating in those days a long, tedious (hazardous too) journey from the mainland port.

Although so far from the mainland, the isle is yet vulnerable to its lure and impact. Young people tend to leave it for the big world, though the old are still there, and a few of the young too, who prefer to stick to the place and its past-oriented life-pattern.

Mark belongs to the race of "white intruders" (*IHO* 23); yet he comes to this remote place, among an alien people, and wins over the Indians day by day, with his hard work, commitment, his sincerity and genuine sharing of their troubles; eventually a time comes when they accept him as one of their own. So, at the end, following his death, the old carver at the edge of the village keeps 'wake', just as he would have done to a dear one of his own tribe.

In a way it is the story of a pilgrim's progress. Mark Brian comes to the bishop's "hardest parish" on the patrol of the Indian villages at Kingcome; renders service there,—not with snobbery, but with love and respect, which has been sadly lacking in most of his fellow-whites, as the author takes care to point out. He learns the Indian's life and ways bit by bit through hard work, and with respect and patient understanding; their social customs, their death-rites, their fests, their values, their sad pride which fails to sustain them any more in the face of a cruel greedy world, which makes its onslaughts by stealing away its treasured ancient masks and lovely young daughters.

The American tourists cannot "tell the Indians apart" (*IHO* 86); Mark too initially could not; but before long Mark knows each one of them and has a special personal word of greeting or kindness to spare for each person entering the church. Slowly, the place, along with its beautiful wild nature as well as the quaint dignified people, seeps into his mind.

When finally the order for transfer arrives, "the thought filled him with a twinge of sudden anguish and fear.... How would he live again in the old world he had almost forgotten?" (*IHO* 125). When Keetah, the daughter of the village, implores him not to leave—"because this is your village and we are your family", Mark does not have words to thank for this recognition and acceptance, "for the sudden, unexpected gift of peace which they had offered him in their quiet, perceptive way" (*IHO* 131).

After his death in the river the village gives him a touching send-off to "the land of the owl," as had been their ancient custom. In a touching gesture Old Peter keeps his 'wake' on the last ledge of the village, in case the dear departed came back in the form of a bird, as a great chief of the tribe was believed to come back after death in the old times; Peter would assure him, "It is only old Peter, the Carver, who waits here, friend" (*IHO* 138).

The Place

a wild, lovely and lonely island....

The charming brief narrative has been woven around the place, i.e. the island, and the island remains the most powerful presence all along.

The place is first introduced through the young outsider's sensory perception. Following Mark on his boat-voyage to Kingcome, the reader enters an obscure queer place. Eventually, it will become his home. But at the beginning it is starkly alien to the newcomer: "The tops of the islands were wreathed in cloud, the sides fell steeply, and the firs that covered them grew so precisely to the high tide line that now, at slack, the up-coast of British Columbia showed its bones in a straight selvage of wet, dark rock" (*IHO* 3-4). It is a stark almost rebuffing scenario that greets the passenger on the boat: "There was no beach…nothing but clean, straight selvage, and a scattered mound of…[clam shells] broken and white in the grey of rain against the green of spruce" (*IHO* 4). On the second night of this passage "There was nothing but a lonely magnificence of sea and islands" (*IHO* 9).

As the boat moves closer to the last stop, it is a primordial scenario, looking ageless in its wild solitude: "...the great mountains lifting into the sky. On the far side of the inlet...a strip of bare granite, like the ragged scar of some huge grizzly, where a slide had peeled off every tree, every bit of soil. ...little falls that cascaded down cliffs, green with moss.... They moved up the twenty-mile inlet with the dusk deepening into dark, the raindrops glistening, falling slowly in the searchlight, an occasional little fish darting through the white, spumy wake off the bow" (*IHO* 10). Later, on the way to consigning the ashes of Calamity to the sea, he will see trees reflected in the water, "that must have been growing when Christ was a little lad" (*IHO* 127).

But Mark also realises on arrival, for the first time in his life, "the stolid, stubborn indifference of the inanimate" (*IHO* 14), as every single thing had to be taken up the river in order to reach the isle village. Ultimately Mark will be killed by some such stubborn, inanimate element on the same river.

Still his arrival is welcomed by a blissful peace of a picturesque scene: serene, cool, exquisite:

> on this, one of the last good days of fall, it was cold, the water calm, and deep green from the shadow of the cedars. The falls slipped down the mossy cliffs. The mountains were snow-tipped... the hand of the Welcome totem rose above the trees, and hundreds of small birds, of ducks and geese, rose at their passing. (*IHO* 15)

Eventually the young vicar will find his own faith in tune with the place, and this is indicated on the day of his first arrival, and performance of the first rite, which is the burial of a child. As he utters his prayer, "it was as if they had been written for this place and this time. When he spoke, 'I will lift up mine eyes unto the hills', there were the mountains rising above the great trees, and when he read that small and lovely prayer, '...protect him all day long until the shadows lengthen and the evening comes....' the sun had slipped beneath the mountain tops, and the shadows were lengthening on the small grave at his feet" (*IHO* 20).

The morning after the funeral "the village was quiet, and utterly at peace" (*IHO* 25), just as nearly two years later, after his own death the village will be "quiet, and at peace" (*IHO* 137).

The rain seems to be a perpetual presence in this place. " In November the rain fell in a slow and patient drizzle" (*IHO* 42). August brings incessant rains and flood. The winter made things particularly difficult. "With December all the things in the village—the stubborn, inanimate things—revolted at once" (*IHO* 43). "When the weather turned cold, the trip up river became torment" (*IHO* 44). Ten days before Christmas Mark and Jim visit the villages, and "each lonely float, in and out the inlets," to deliver the gifts, "travelling usually with the compass, often with the bow awash, and always with the mountains thick with snow" (*IHO* 46). During the January storms one cannot reach from one island to another for a month. However, in due course the winter is over, and spring bursts in. Craven lovingly mentions how "with spring the first buds began to swell, and the fresh green needles of the spruce. The bracken and the fern reached out the tips of tender fronds, the devil's club put out small new leaves for the deer to nibble, and the bears emerged from their dens, thin, blinking in the light" (*IHO* 68). But again the lovely summer days yield place to ceaseless rain, followed by the fall. "Fall came gently with the second blooming of the dogwood. No wind blew, the clouds hung over the village, and the rains were soft" (*IHO* 101). "Slowly, as the needles fell, the waters of the inlet grew less clear, and on the river floated the first green leaves of the alders. When the nights cooled, the little berry bush burned crimson under the great, dark cedar, and on one deep green island side, a single cottonwood turned gold" (*IHO* 102).

Fall "flowed past the village like the river" (*IHO* 105), and Christmas arrives once again. In January the village is ice-bound and no boat can come or go. Before long it will be followed by the spring, with its heavy rains, along with the catastrophe. The pilgrim's progress is mapped out along the course of the seasonal cycle, which again is rapidly rushing things onward for the doom awaiting the young man, and ultimately the ancient island.

Flora and Fauna

Every season brings its own special gifts to the island, in terms of sound and colour. The place comes alive with its wealth of flora and fauna, even before the humans make their appearance on the scene. The animals, big and small, move about regally, unafraid of humans. The book opens with the "doomed man" Mark, with only two years at his disposal, entering the island in a boat: he stands at the wheel, watching the stream, "and the bald eagles fishing for herring that waited until the boat was almost upon them to lift, to drop the instant it had passed"

(*IHO* 3). During his passage to Kingcome "a school of porpoise refused to move out of the boat's way, and watched the boat, heads up, headed straight for the boat, and at the last moment, leapt aside" (*IHO* 8). "Two small racoons, making a strange whirring sound, begged Mark for bread and took it gently in their strange little hands" (*IHO* 9). He feels he is entering a 'strange' land, and its strangeness is accentuated by its landscape, its flora and fauna. When he comes close to the last inlet, Mark sees "the dorsal fin of a killer whale cruising slowly down the far side" (9). Mark collides with "a huge dark shape" (*IHO* 46) in the darkness of night prior to Christmas; a bear attracted by the unfamiliar sound of the church organ.

The burst of early spring is described in terms of flowers and birds, with attention to accurate details. With the advent of spring, rains having softened, the winds lightened, "the eagles and robins returned to the village. High in the skyways wild geese called exultantly on their first early passages back from the south, the wise old crow cawed over the river, his wings flapping loosely and slowly, and the sleek black raven, who stayed all year, nested in the tall alders" (*IHO* 68). It is also the season of fishing; Mark accompanies a fishing team to king's inlet, "a wild, lovely and lonely land, the boat rolling in the tidal sweep, the seals disputing each fish" (*IHO* 68).

The passage of human life here seems to be in perfect harmony with the nature around. As the vicar and the pall-bearers proceed along the deep shadowy narrow path, the dark firs shedding wet drops from the last rain on their heads, "an eagle accompanied them, soaring and returning in great, wide arcs, and once they surprised a doe and her little fawn... the tribe stretched through the cedar and the hemlock, coming slowly and silently, except for the footfalls on the soft duff. ...the air fresh from the rain and filled with the sweet smell of fir, the sky blue and white with cloud. On the top of Whoop-Szo...snow lay waiting for the warm...July to send it sliding downward..." (*IHO* 71).

Mark himself will die from such a slide at the end. Anyway, at this moment it seemed to Mark that "death belonged here as the mountain belonged, as the eagle belonged, and the little scurrying squirrels that peered at him from the fir boughs. And it seemed to him that the ugliness of death was as unimportant here as the fir needles which made the path soft beneath his feet, or last year's windfall in the thick underbrush" (*IHO* 72). This place is going to serve an appropriate serene 'prelude';

is it preparing him for his own death, already waiting by the wings, though he does not know yet.

The following morning the weary vicar is seen sitting beside the old matriarch on a log by the river's edge, both silent, "listening to the mewing of the gulls, watching two sleek black ravens in the alders across the river" (*IHO* 73). With fall, "the land belonged first to the wild fowl...the loud calling of the first immense flocks of snow geese, ...the black brants passing high over the village like a long whisper, like a sigh" (*IHO* 102).

The flora, the fauna, and the elements together create the music of the island. On the last night of his first passage to Kingcome the young vicar wakes up; through the open porthole of his cabin "he could hear the wind murmuring in the firs, and the distant mewing of the gulls" (*IHO* 11). By his first November here "already the rain had become an element of life like the air Mark breathed, and when it stopped, he missed it somehow, and found himself listening for the drip, drip, drip that seemed now a necessary and comforting component of his life" (*IHO* 42). Through the nights of August Mark hears "the drip-drip of the rain, which had become a part of life itself, so that when it ceased, the world was filled suddenly with a strange, unnatural silence" (*IHO* 85). It will be another night of rain and thunder that Mark will meet his end on the river, his boat being struck by a rumbling landslide, whose explosive sound will send the signal through the village.

People

> They lived where they had always lived. They fished as they had always fished,...
>
> It was loneliness that Indians had lived through all the centuries, and it was in loneliness Mark came to know them best.

"Here every bird and fish knew its course" (*IHO* 102) through the seasons, the author elaborates, "every tree had its own place upon this earth. Only man had lost his way. Then, when the geese had passed, and the bear and the little hibernating animals had hidden themselves for their long sleep, the white trunks of the alders stood stripped and stark across the river, and man began to emerge, to prove again his capacity for endurance and faithfulness. It was in loneliness the Indians had lived through all the centuries, and it was in loneliness Mark came to know them best" (*IHO* 102-03).

I Heard the Owl is depiction of a place and its people who are tradition-bound; though already caught up in the process of change, they cling to the last vestiges of a past, its ways, beliefs, rituals, myth,—all in tune with the island they live in, and have lived for generations. "They lived where they had always lived. They fished as they had always fished, known for their intelligence and a culture that was perhaps the most highly developed of any native band of the continent" (*IHO* 3).

They are proverbially known as a people "born with a paddle and a fish hook in...hand" (90). When Keetah's family leave the village all of a sudden Mark is worried, how will they leave. Jim says nonchalantly: "As my people have always lived. They will live on fish, and clams, and seaweed. Later they will pick berries" (*IHO* 61).

It is through Mark's eyes that the reader sees this people. Mark thinks in the early days, "Indians belonged here as the birds and fish belonged; …he was a guest in their house, and he knew, also, that this might never change" (*IHO* 29). Initially, when he felt "he was a guest in their house", all faces looked alike to Mark too; but with time he knew better. After months of stay he writes to his Bishop: "I have learned little of the Indians as yet. I know only what they are not. They are none of the things one has been led to believe. They are not simple, or emotional, they are not primitive" (*IHO* 45).

By the end of the year, on the Christmas morning, after completing all the arrangements for the morning service, Mark "stepped into one of those moments that is suspended between time and space and lingers in the mind. The snow lay thick on the shoulders of the Cedar man; the limbs of the young spruce bent beneath its weight"; and then he saw the tribe coming up slowly with the flickering lanterns. He wonders: "How many times had they travelled through the mountain passes down from the Bering Sea?" (*IHO* 46). He goes to the door, opens it, and greets each by his name. "For the first time he knew them for what they were... and...how deep was his commitment to them" (46).

Mark is marked by a fineness, dignity, and trustful simplicity which are also the hallmark of these people in general. The elders talk together, in one voice, in sad monotone, like the Greek chorus, articulating their fears anxieties, sorrows of the community, and making forecasts, replete with anxiety and wishful thinking.

Mark was warned by the island-expert Caleb: "They will all watch you" (*IHO* 4). His boatman Jim, Caleb warned: "could handle a boat when he was ten, and he knows more about the coast than you will ever learn" (4); Caleb also informs, he is not shy; he is watchful; silent, watchful—all of them. Is it suspicion? Apprehension? Mistrust? Or suspicious distance? "In his eyes you'll see a look that is in the eyes of all of them, and it will be your job to figure out what it means.... And he will watch you—they will all watch you—and in his own time he will accept or reject you" (4).

Yet, they are easily cheated, simple and uncalculating as they always have been. "They do not budget what they have, and even when times are excellent, they get into debt. It is then the dealers pick up their best carvings" (*IHO* 64-65).

There is no history of open animosity with the white outsider, though there are instances of clan hostility. "The tribes...belonged to a people that had never been at war with the white man" (6). But they have their innocent small pride; for instance, Mrs Hudson's "small revenge on the white man, the intruder" by serving them mashed turnips (*IHO* 23). But sometimes the resentment can be guessed. When Keetah's family have been put on disgrace by a white youth, Mrs Hudson, the old matriarch lifts her proud old face and says slowly to Mark: "What have you done to us? What has the white man done to our young?" (*IHO* 62).

They lead a life of continuity; the old ways are retained as much as possible in this farflung island. But the extraordinary degree of pride and arrogance of the older days were gone.

People: Customs

Jim tells Mark during his first passage to Kingcome: "On the cliffs before you reach the river, you will see paintings of cattle, sheep, goats and coppers that mark the gifts given in a great tribal potlatch" (*IHO* 11). The potlatch was considered a great event in the locality, and the ancient custom was followed as late as the 1930s. Later Mark will learn about the local customs day by day: the professional mourners who take turns wailing day and night, when somebody dies (*IHO* 16); that they have no written language; that during a burial after the Christian rites are over, an elder takes over and performs in the ancient Kwákwala which the young no longer knew (*IHO* 21); the ceremonial masks made with the real hair of ancestors—"as if…a strong, proud, living face, so beautifully was it carved" (53); the traditional community dances with the masks on (*IHO* 56) where no outsider and no photography are allowed. When the women lament it is with "a strange little sound that must have come down through the centuries in chant of sorrow" (*IHO* 54-55). They are ashamed of one who marries a white man (*IHO* 55).

Old customs show the isladers' respect for the river and the fish. In late March the tribe got ready for the coming of the candlefish; by holding community feast, and the elders recounting the various myths about óolachon, the candlefish.

> ...the times Mark liked best were the long summer twilights when the elders dropped in to speak of the old culture. They were all alike, the old, tied by a common bond. 'We are the only ones left to remember the old ways and if we do not speak now, they will be forgotten'. Sometimes Mark was appalled at how much was gone, how little they remembered from their long past. (77)

Collective fishing in the summer night, and the boisterous happiness also form part of this custom "These were the lovely days of summer; the water of the inlet deep green from the shadows of the spruce, the children in and out of the river all day long, agile as seals, and the village full of laughter" (*IHO* 80).

On the other hand, an event of death or birth is shared by all. When Gordon's mother dies of her sixth childbirth, "everyone in the village shared the death" (*IHO* 70), women preparing food for the guests to come, men digging the grave in the burial ground, older boys assisting them, children preparing wreaths, old women cleaning the church. It is by sharing their sorrows and joys as one of them that Mark becomes accepted in course of time.

People: Hunting

> At star-fall a young buck walked through the village to drink at the river. He was unafraid of guns.

The animals are held in respect, though hunting is part of their livinghood. "At star-fall a young buck walked through the village to drink at the river. He was unafraid of guns. The Indians hunted for food, not for fun, and when he found it necessary to kill a deer, he did not shoot him. If possible, he knocked him over the head with a club" (*IHO* 25).

Once Mark goes with the hunting team up on the mountain; prior to this he has joined their fishing party. Thus slowly friendship was forged between them, "without words and needing none", on jungle paths and river-side, where hunting and fishing took place (41).

"The tide dominated all life". When the tide was out, clamming was on. When clamming was on, all else waited, even church (*IHO* 56). The men never talk loudly of the hunt that was planned lest the game hears and goes in hiding (*IHO* 39). All this denotes a primordial way of life close to nature, with its innate wisdom, restraint, and respect for animals even when one is forced to kill.

People: Sadness

A strange sadness seems to hang upon the look and mood of the islanders. On coming out to the deck on his first morning on the boat Mark finds his pilot Jim, a local youth of twenty-seven, his age, "waited patiently as if he had waited all his life, as if he were part of time itself" (*IHO* 6). There was pride in his eyes without arrogance. Behind the pride was "a sadness so deep it seemed to stretch back into ancient mysteries Mark could not even imagine" (*IHO* 7). The author throws in a hint of Mark's initial thrill at the challenge.

Later, on the day of his first arrival, Mark notes with surprise the same expression in the face of Christ's picture inside the church: "His face was the Indian's face, His eyes the Indian eyes and in them the depth of sadness" (*IHO* 16).

On his first morning in the island Mark meets a bereaved mother waiting for her child's burial. "She waited as if she had waited all her life, as if she were part of time itself, gently and patiently". In the old days it could have been different.

Eventually, the same look comes to settle down upon Mark's face as well. Later on, when Mark has come closer to them, when he comes to learn about the ruin and death of Keetah's sister, "he did not know that…in his own eyes was the depth of sadness which he had begun to understand" (*IHO* 67). He has begun to imbibe the spirit of the place.

Myth

The myths are the village.

The people appreciate the new vicar's respect for their custom which was shown by his silent withdrawal from the graveside when they had followed up Christian rites by their own pagan rituals; but they are apprehensive about their own young generation,—"we are losing our sons, and...our young no longer understand the meaning of the totems" (*IHO* 23).

The author carefully picks up local myths, customs, ways which are already on the way to oblivion; expectedly, the wild nature of their isle, the animals around—the whale, the wolf, the boulder-sliding 'Noisy Mountain', the 'Cedar Man', the 'man-god who lived in the sea', the salmon—populate this twilight mythic world of an ancient sea-encircled island.

On the last leg of Mark's first passage to Kingcome the boat slips through a pass so narrow that Mark fears they should scrape on the rock; "the huge rock shaped like a whale and covered with brown seaweed" (*IHO* 10). Jim informs him that his people call it 'Whale Pass', "because long ago the gods turned a whale into that rock" (10). Lying awake in his cabin on the eve of reaching the destination Mark recalls what the Bishop had told him about the village, the myth of its genesis:

> It is an old village—nobody knows how old. According to the myth, after the great flood two brothers were the only human beings left alive in the world, and they heard a voice speak and it said, 'Come, Wolf, lend your skin that they may go fleetly and find themselves a home'. And in the wolf's skin the brothers moved south until they came to a small and lovely valley on a river's edge, surrounded by high mountains, and here they returned the skin to their friend, the wolf, and...the elder built his house, and in his dances he moved right as even now the dancers move right because the wolf moved right, and on his totem he carved a wolf as one of the crests of his tribe. (*IHO* 11)

Myths and customs thus go hand in hand here, constituting their life.

There are also other natural protectors of the tribe, who are celebrated in their myth; as the Bishop had told him: "according to the tribal history its site was chosen wisely because the river, its access, is treacherous and easily defended" (*IHO* 12); but when the wiser enemy came through a mountain pass and down the river, then "the spirit that lives in Whoop-Szo, the Noisy Mountain, that is across the river and towers over the village, heard the enemy coming and sent down a slide and buried it" (*IHO* 12).

"And a voice said to the great cedar tree in Bond Sound, 'Come forth, Tzakamayi and be a man', and he came forth to be the Cedar-man, the first man-god of the people and more powerful than all others" (13). During the hunting season at night in the shake cabins "the Indians talked so long of the man-god who lived in the sea and controlled the sea" that Mark went to sleep before he ever leaned what the killer whale said to the swimmer, and the swimmer to the halibut (*IHO* 41).

Though by the time of the story Kingcome is a "compact, Christian village" (12), the myths are still alive in the memory and consciousness of the elders. But the young, who get education in the mainland, are getting alienated; as Old Peter worries: "They do not remember the myths, and the meaning of the totems" (52). After listening to the myth of the now forbidden frenzied Hamatsa dance, and its terrifying impact, Mark wonders:

> How had it been in the old days when the magic, and supernatural spirits, and the cannibal man who lived at the north end of the world had dominated life here in this village? How had it been when the hamatsa had come in the night through the great trees, crying his soft and terrible call? He would never know. No man would ever know. But Mark had seen the light of the old, old ways reflected on the faces like the glow from a dying campfire, and he knew that it was the hamatsa who had been freed at last from his holy madness, and was at peace in the deep woods. (*IHO* 101)

The unavoidable reality that stares in the face of the islanders is that their myths and rituals are dying out one by one.

Decadence

> They belonged to…the self-exiles of this earth, clinging fiercely to a way that is almost gone, as the last leaves fall at last gently and with great pride,
>
> …but in the end it will be deserted, the totem will fall, and the green will cover them.

In spite of her love and appreciation of the islandscape which she articulates through the sensitive and sometimes rapturous response of Mark, the young vicar from the big world outside, Craven does not fail to note the overriding presence of decadence, which has already set in. Like the vicar, who is terminally ill, the island too is doomed; it is rapidly decaying, and unlike the active young man, it is counting its last days passively.

The shadow of death seems to hang over and around this place. On the second afternoon of his passage, he approaches the first village of his patrol. "First you will see Ghost Island. It is where the Indians of Gilford village once buried their dead...in low sheds. Most of them have fallen and broken" (*IHO* 7). Jim adds an eerie detail: "If you go there now, you stumble over skulls green with moss" (8). The dead have been, as it were, undergoing a second death. Yet it is beautiful in its own way. Mark sees "the small island, lovely as a jade jewel,...with its rare beach, white with clam cells, its stretch of cedar houses facing the water, and four great cedar posts standing in the rain—all that was left of some ancient ceremonial house" (*IHO* 8). Two carved killer whales mark the grave of Johnny Ray who was drowned; and Johnny is supposed to be a lively ghost , hiding in the bush, stealing things, and scaring women (8).

On the day of his first arrival Mark is faced with an event of death, the body of a dead child, waiting for burial. While proceeding towards the burial ground at the other end of the isle, Mark meets signs of decay strewn about by the path: "the battered eagle poised on a slender shaft. One totem pole was so old he could discern only the top figure, a bear wearing at a most jaunty angle the lid of a garbage can to keep him from weathering further" (19-20). Even the grave trees have decayed, with sheds and carvings crumbling down. In the old days each family had its own trees, Mark is informed, on which the boxes were hoisted by ropes and tied one above another in the tops. "Many have fallen as you can see, and the grave sheds that were built later have fallen and most of the old carvings" (*IHO* 20).

As he enters the vicarage at the end of the first day, it is stepping "into the sweet and spicy smell of death" (*IHO* 22). However, after a few weeks he will not find "the sweet smell of death [not] too oppressive" (*IHO* 28). Anyway, even "the vicarage was falling down" (27), with the tower broken, the place dank and cold, papers hanging in shreds from the walls which were discoloured and warped by seeping rain, the window sills coming loose, and the floor sagging beneath one's feet.

After Christmas Mark feels "a strange wind of dissent whispering through the firs" (51); he asks old Peter the carver. The old man answers: "It is always so the young come back from school. My people are proud of them, and resent them" (52). "Here in the village my people are at home as the fish in the sea, as the eagle in the sky" (*IHO* 52). But the white-educated young are drifting away. "When the young leave", Peter continues, "the world takes them, and damages them…. They go, and soon the village will go also" (52). Mark tries to assure him, "Kingcome will be one of the last to go, Peter". But Peter has no illusions: "Yes, but in the end it will be deserted, the totem will fall, and the green will cover them. And when I think of it, I am glad I will not be here to see" (*IHO* 52). The old order is going to die out with the dying generation.

True, some are desperately trying to hold out, but it is holding out to the inevitable.

Keetah's family leave the village in shame as their daughter had eloped with a white man who, to add further injury to insult, had secured the giant mask of the isle by cheat, the narrator comments: "They were larger than themselves. They belonged to the great and small hegiras of the self-exiles of this earth, clinging fiercely to a way that is almost gone, as the last leaves fall at last gently and with great pride" (*IHO* 62).

When the young leave for Vancouver schools, none of them knew "he was leaving his boyhood behind and would not find it again. But the old knew it. The old knew this was another bit of the slow dying of all they held dear in their own race" (*IHO* 91). Gordon represents a typical case; after his city-schooling the boy admits: "I can never come home again" (*IHO* 106). But Keetah at least comes back. She has realised "my village is the only place I know myself" (*IHO* 118).

There is no sentimentalizing anyway. In his last advice to Jim on the fatal night Mark tells Jim: "each year take her (his wife) outside until it is familiar to her. Someday, when the village is no more, you too must cross the bridge" (*IHO* 132).

Carnival

> The community feast was held...the women began the dancing... turning right because the wolf turns right.

Under the shadow of decadence and death their simple carnival takes place on occasions, which usually makes them drunk and sometimes vulnerable too on that account. Jim reports one such experience on this Ghost Island: "We had some fine dancing, the air filled with duck down. We saw the famous blanket trimmed with a thousand eagle beaks, and because we are not permitted to buy liquor to serve in our own homes, the boys traded two masks for three cases of beer, and we drank it very fast and got very drunk" (*IHO* 8).

The traditional mask-dances (*IHO* 57-58),—the Wolf Dance, the Grouse Dance, the Moon Dance, followed by potlatch which included feast and gifts; obviously these dances were closely related to their life. Jim explains the Grouse Dance to Mark: "If you were an Indian walking beside a stream in the woods, knowing the woods as only an Indian knows them, everything you saw would come to life in this dance with all its meaning and its beauty" (58). But the old carnivals too are on the wane. The big dance-potlatches are now forbidden, but nothing has come up to replace it. Jim laments, "They were the great rituals of my people, solemn and important. Now the meaning is gone" (*IHO* 59). During the festival a village mask is 'sold' under liquor, and a village girl is seduced away by a white man from outside. The girl's family leave the village out of shame. The girl will be thrown out later by her lover, and will end by slow suicide.

Anyway, the family come back after the lapse of a period. Then in fishing season one afternoon "the village was filled with the fragrance of the salmon barbecuing on the alder fires. The community feast was held...the women began the dancing...turning right because the wolf turns right" (*IHO* 83), thereby invoking the ancient myth of the locale.

The Island-village

> This is the village. If you go there, from the time you tie up at the float in the inlet, the village is you.

How do the people look at their island-village? The Bishop beautifully introduces the village to the would-be-comer, in a sustained prose-poem, in the tone of a folk-saga:

> The Indian knows his village and feels for his village as no white man for his country, his town, or even for his own bit of land. His village is not the strip of land four miles long and three miles wide that is his as long as the sun rises and the moon sets. The myths are the village, and the winds and rains. The river is the village and the black and white killer whales.... The village is the salmon who comes up the river to spawn, the seal who follows the salmon and bites off its head, the bluejay whose name is like the sound he makes—'Kwiss-Kwiss'. The village is the talking bird, the owl, who calls the name of the man who is going to die, and the silver-tipped grizzly who ambles into the village, and the little white speck that is the mountain goat on Whoop-Szo. The fifty-foot totem by the church is the village, and the Cedar-man, who stands at the bottom holding up the eagle, the wolf and the raven!" (*IHO* 12-13)

The Bishop concludes "This is the village. If you go there, from the time you tie up at the float in the inlet, the village is you" (13).

Mark has to go the Indian way, doing bit by bit with his own hands, and eventually he wins their respect. At the year's end the Bishop writes to him: "You have suffered with them, and now you are theirs" (*IHO* 74). By sharing their sorrow Mark becomes one of them, accepted. Simultaneously, he gets alienated from the outside world. So, when the August outsiders,—insensitive, haughty, arrogant snobs—leave at last, he feels glad; "They were on their way back to a life he no longer knew, as distant as a planet" (87). These casual or curious tourists serve to highlight the uniqueness of Mark's response vis-à-vis the place. When Mark meets his city-friends, during his brief stop at Vancouver he realises "with a shock that he no longer talked the same language" (*IHO* 92).

In order to assure Gordon on his first embarkation Mark tells him: "I was lonely, and I was afraid when I went to your village" (*IHO* 95). But now this is his home. When he returns to the isle after a brief absence, he feels "the quickening...growing eagerness of one who comes home" (94) after a long absence; and he eagerly notes the landmarks as the familiar features on a dear face (94). When he bids good-bye to some loggers, whom he had briefly accompanied up the river, "he felt somehow that he had known these staunch and kindly people…all his life" (*IHO* 126).

When the Bishop offers replacement Mark wonders: "How would he live again in the old world he had almost forgotten...? Here, where death waited behind each tree, he had made friends with loneliness, with death and deprivation..." (*IHO* 125).

In the face of oncoming death Mark knows with humility, "he had learned a little of the truth of one tribe in one village. He had seen the sadness, the richness, the tragic poignancy of a way of life that each year, bit by bit, slipped beyond memory and was gone. For a time he had been part of it, one of the small unknown men who take their stand in some remote place, and fight out their battle in a quiet way" (*IHO* 125). A deep spiritual conviction conditions his 'battle'.

On the return journey, after consigning the ashes of Calamity to the sea "all day long he moved down the longest, the loveliest of all the inlets, and it seemed to him "time had lost its contours"; no future, no present; "he seemed to see it as the raven or the bald eagle, flying high over the village, must see the part of the river that had passed the village..." (*IHO* 127). On reaching the vicarage he hears the owl; he tells Marta, "on the bank of the river I heard the owl call my name"; and Marta says, "Yes, my son" (129); because, she knows. Mark feels he would rather die here than move on: "How could he return now to that far country he no longer knew, where, while awaiting death, he would be a stranger?" (*IHO* 129).

The Swimmer

You are the swimmer who came to us from the great sea.

Mark came here along the tide, rowing his canoe. In course of the story Mark becomes identified with the 'swimmer' in the islanders' perception.

Before coming here Mark had read in some book, they spoke with respect of salmon, and called him 'swimmer'. During a fishing trip Jim shows him the 'swimmer's coming from the sea into the clear river water in order to spawn. The narrator gives an elaborate description of the coming as if it were a great event. Mark watches fascinated at the run,—two to three feet beneath the surface—"hundreds of silvery fish, pressed tight, moving…stealthily, with a kind of desperate urgency" (34). All of a sudden he starts chanting: "Come, swimmer,… I am glad to be alive now that you have come to this good place where we can play together. Take this sweet food…younger brother" (34). Jim is surprised how could the outsider know this. It is the prayer Jim's people used to offer to the salmon in ancient times. Jim recalls his grandfather doing the same. Jim also tells him of the inevitable end of the swimmer: "in the end the swimmer dies, and the river takes him downstream, tail first, as he started" (35). Mark wants to see the end. So at the end of the season one day they creep to the edge of the stream and look down.

"They watched her last valiant fight for life, her struggle to right herself when the gentle stream turned her, and they watched the water force open her gills and draw her slowly downstream, tail first, as she had started to the sea as a fingerling" (37). Keetah is saddened; but Mark consoles her; the argument he uses would apply no less to his own coming here with one tide and leaving on another after accomplishing his mission: "The whole life of the swimmer is one of courage and adventure. All of it builds to the climax and the end. When the swimmer dies he has spent himself completely for the end for which he was made, and this is not sadness. It is triumph" (37). Is he himself aware of the parallel? Anyway, the hints are there. Old Marta recalls when she was a child, twins born in the village were supposed to be not really children, but 'swimmers' (37); Mark tells them of his twin sister, who happens to be his only close relative; at this all laugh, and Marta says, "The swimmer is your relative. You belong to the salmon people" (38).

Thereafter, "whenever they came up the river from the float, Mark watched for the swimmer, the pressed silver forms moving secretly beneath the surface" (38). Though he does not see him again, somehow a subtle connection has been established between the two.

Even earlier, prior to his setting out for Kingcome, Caleb had coached Mark about handling the forty-foot diesel launch "upon which his life would depend" (5), which seems ironically proleptic in retrospective view; because it is in this boat that he will meet death at the end. Caleb advises him to keep the tide-book open beside the compass, "because you came with the tide, you went with the tide, you waited for the tide, and sometimes you prayed for the tide" (5). Very much like the 'swimmer' indeed!

Towards the end when the owl has already called his name, and the villagers know its purport, because Marta has been told by the Bishop, they write to the Bishop to let him remain here to the end. They entreat: "because this is your village and we are your family. You are the swimmer who came to us from the great sea" (*IHO* 131).

The end comes the very same day. On being asked to assist in the search for a lost young logger, who had drunk too much in the beer parlour, stolen a motor boat, and disappeared. The escapee is spotted before long. But while returning Mark meets the end. It is one of those thunderous spring rains; the lightning strikes a tree on inlet top, which falls upon others below, leading to a landslide. The boat is caught in the slide and is wrecked. Keetah would have called out, like her great-great-grandmother on a similar crisis, "called upon all the gods, the guardian spirits of the tribe, to help her. 'Come wolf, come swimmer! Come raven, come eagle'" (*IHO* 134). But no help comes.

The closing of the narration quivers with the resonance of pagan rites emotionally re-lived. As the canoes, bringing the dead back, appear at the river's bend "the old people began a chant of sorrow in the ancient language which the young no longer knew. 'Aie-aie-aie—he has left us—aie-aie-aie', until even the breeze seemed to whisper it, and the trees to sigh of it" (*IHO* 137). As the men take their turns to carry the body to the black sands, "the women sang an ancient hymn to a Supreme Being whose existence had been sensed before the white men had ever come to this land" (137).

The Lord's Prayer is joined by the tribe's own chant. In the night the entire village goes dark except the one lantern in the small church.

The island-village remembers and performs the last rites to its dear 'swimmer' in their age-old fashion, lovingly sadly, endearingly:

> In her house old Marta lay awake in the dark, and she said softly, "Walk straight on, my son. Do not look back. Do not turn your head. You are going to the land of our Lord." (137)
>
> In the last house of the village, Peter, the carver, lay awake also, and he remembered that in the old days when a great chief died, his soul came straight back to the village in the sleek black body of a raven...Peter did not believe this literally. Yet it seemed likely to him that the soul of the young vicar would return to the village he had loved, as would his own, and surely it would be most inhospitable if no one was awake and waiting. Thus he dressed and sat on the top step of his house in the dark night, and hearing the rustle of some small night creature he, too, spoke softly, "It is only old Peter, the carver, who waits here, friend". (*IHO* 138)

The concluding paragraph, which is made in one long sentence, again evokes the swimmer,

> Past the village flowed the river, like time, like life itself, waiting for he swimmer to come again on his way to the climax of his adventurous life, and to the end for which he has been made.... That is all. (138)

The suggestion is apparent.

In an adequate gesture Craven has dedicated her book to "the Tsawataineuk tribe at Kingcome village, B.C."

Beverly Slapin, in his review of the book writes: "Craven's writing is spare, simple, and beautiful, with understanding and compassion." "It is possible for an author to put down, in truth and beauty, the lives of a people not her own. Such authors are few and far between. Margaret Craven is one of them."

Regarding story element as such there is little. The narrator, who is neither critical nor analytical in her presentation of the islandscape, consistently follows a Biblical style—simple, sparse, eloquent, often incremental in its repetitive nuances. The narrative is simple, rhythmic like the dripping rain, almost monotonous, yet charming in its attuning with the life it narrates. At every step and turn the author tries to remember and remind the reader of the past, by continuously relating the present to a distant past, and thereby underscoring the fragility of the present in this "small and lovely island" (36).

NOTE

1. J.E. Housman, in his "Introduction" to *Popular English Ballads*, observes: "On the whole, the ballad is in sympathy with the outlaw, the mosstrooper, the poacher, as long as he does not show wanton cruelty, lack of sympathy with the poor, or licentiousness. There is a sturdy sense of the value of the individual as opposed to the unjust encroachments of Government in these ballads, as there is manifest delight in the individual or group of individuals at bay" (Housman 1952:20).

WORKS CITED

Benson, E. *J.M. Synge*. NY: Grove Press, 1982.

Bourgeois, M. *John M. Synge and the Irish Theatre*. NY: Blom, 1965.

Burlands, C., Nicholson, I., Osborne, H. *Mythology of the Americas.* (London; N.Y.: Hamlyn Publishing Group, 1970), 22-47.

Craven, M. *I Heard the Owl Call My Name.* Toronto: Clarke, Irwin and Co. Ltd., 1967. [mentioned as *IHO*]

Greene, David H. and Edward M. Stephens. *J.M. Synge*. NY: The Macmillan Company, 1959.

Foote, T. "A Swimmer's Tale" (Review of *IHO*). *Time Magazine*, 28 Jan. 1974. Vol. 103, p. 73.

Hadley, Michael. *God's Little Ships: A History of the Columbia Coast Mission*. Madeira Park, B.C.: Harbour Publishing, 1990.

Liammóir, Micheál Mac. "Introduction". *John Millington Synge: Plays, Poems, Prose.* London: Everyman's Library, 1941; rpt. 1972.

Murray, Christopher. "Unlocking Synge Today", in *A Companion to Modern British and Irish Drama, 1880-2005* [ed. Mary Luckhurst]. Oxford: Wiley-Blackwell, 2010.

Niven, F.J. "Canada" *People of All Nations*, II (Ed. J.A. Hammerton). London: Educational Book Co. Ltd., N.D.

Skelton, Robin. *The Writings of J.M. Synge*. London: Thames and Hudson, 1971.

Slapin, Beverly (http://americanindiansinchildrensliterature. blogspot.in/2007/09/margaret-cravens-i-heard-owl-call-my.html).

Synge, J.M. *The Aran Islands* (Dublin, Maunsel & Co., Ltd.1907); [* I have used the 1907 edition of the book, as scanned and redacted at sacred-texts.com.] http://www.sacred-texts.com/neu/celt/tai/tai01-taio6.htm cited as (*s-t.ai.*)

Synge, J.M. *Plays, Poems, Prose.* London: J.M. Dent & Sons Ltd., 1941; 4pt. 1954.

Yeats, W.B. *Essays and Introductions*. London.

❑❑❑

The Distinctive Culture and Literary Uniqueness of Mizoram

C. SANGLUAII

LIKE all human communities, the Mizos have their own distinctive culture and society. It has features in common with tribal groups living in the hills of North East India, Burma and South East Asia, including the Philippines and Indonesia. But it is quite different from the Buddhist, Hindu and Islamic cultures of her neighbours. For a long time before the advent of the British, the Mizo people were isolated in the hills of what we know today as 'Mizoram'. This isolation resulted in the development of a unique culture and literature, unaffected by surrounding cultures. Ethno-culturally, the Mizos are strikingly similar to the tribes of South East Asia, while politically and constitutionally they are the sons of India.

The Mizos are a very distinctive people, rich in age-old traditions, culture and heritage of their own. They are rich in folktales, legends, folklore, folksongs and folkmusic. Their traditional values, beliefs and practices have given them a distinctive Mizo identity. The Mizos valued bravery as characteristic of a warring and hunting community which they onced were. Their other values centered round a highly developed and advanced ethical Mizo Code of Conduct known as 'Tlawmngaihna' that marked 'Selflessness', 'devotion to other', 'respect for others', 'Self-denial', 'Service before self' and 'othermindedness'. Every Mizo is expected to abide by this 'Tlawmngaihna' which is a "highly prized" virtue and a "wonderful philosophy of life" which is so rich in meaning and so wide in scope. Mizoram, formerly known as Lushai Hills, came under the British rule in 1890. Mizoram is a hilly region, situated in the North Eastern corner of India and bounded by Myanmar in the east and south, Bangladesh in the west. Towards the North are Assam and Manipur covering an area of 21,087 sq km. The introduction of British rule and arrival of Christian Missionaries in the hills of Mizoram had brought about remarkable changes in the social and cultural life of the people within a short period of time. Before the coming of British missionaries, the Mizos possessed a set of beliefs among which were the belief in 'evil spirits' and belief in 'other worlds', called 'Mitthikhua' the 'dead men's abode' and 'pialral', the paradise for the chosen few. The Mizos also practised animal sacrifice to appease evil spirits and observed three principal festivals; 'Chapchar Kut' in early March after slashing jungles for jhumming, 'Mimkut' in early September after getting the first harvest of Maize and vegetables, and 'Pawlkut' in December after harvesting paddy. Community feasts, singing, dancing and drinking rice beer marked the observance of festivals.

Under the influence of British Missionaries most of the Mizos were converted to Christians within a short period of time. Under the influence of Christianity, the customs and belief in the existence of 'evil spirit', 'head-hunting', 'Zawlbuk' (Bachelors dormitory) disappeared gradually. With Christianity the Mizos gained education, modern ways of life, Western culture, etc., but in exchange of the transformation of their own social life, good old customs, practices, habits, faiths, etc., to a considerable extent. Christianity is therefore supposed to have caused a tremendous impact on the life of the Mizos. The impact of Christianity can be studied from the perspectives of social, cultural, economic, literature and political life of the people. Mass conversion of Mizo people to Christianity and a new concept of Salvation by the grace of God did something to mobilize the will of the people to work out a more sustainable and rewarding existence.

The literature of Mizos has slowly developed after they became Christians. Now, it is regarded that 100% of the Mizos are Christians and as a result there is a great tendency to develop Christian culture, and with the coming of Christianity, development in the field of education is remarkable. During the first decade of the twentieth century considerable progress had been made in opening out Mizoram and bringing the people into contact with Western civilization. The introduction of British rule in Mizoram, therefore, had brought about notable changes in the social and cultural life of the people within a short period of time. As a result, within a short span of time, the chief-oriented society was converted into a Christian-oriented society on the pattern of Western culture. Anyway, the introduction of British rule since 1890 and arrival of Missionaries brought about remarkable cultural and socio-economic change in both rural and urban Mizoram at the cost of old value system in the society. Along with the development and the growth of modern technology, we

Mizos, still have a tendency to preserve, value and appreciate our folk literatures and old customs and practices.

The Mizo Folktales were most widely read as a mere interesting story which is passing on from mouth to mouth by our forefathers and by our grandmothers. Here, I would like to mention one of the most unique and interesting folktales of Mizos, what we called 'Chemtatrawta'. This tale is quite exceptional, known to the Mizos of all ages which proves its uniqueness amongst all. Chemtatrawta, one of the most well-verse tales till today and may be the only folktale in Mizo which can rightly be classified as a cumulative tale. The structure of Chemtatrawta tale is like a Ladder, which takes us a step further, makes the reader to anticipate and keen to know what is going on to happen next, until it reaches its climax. The story begins from the lobster, then Chemtatrawta the hero of the tale moving on to Kha-um (a fruit of a climbing plant) wild fowl, Taivang (kind of big ants), wild boar, bat, elephant, and an old woman. From the old woman it goes back to the reverse step tracing back every step and ended back to the lobster. This kind of tale keeps the reader in suspense which has a humorous approach and becomes popular of all ages.

It is a fact that most of the Mizos are interested in reading Mizo folklore as the Mizo folklore is full of interesting accounts of men's folk and women's folk. For example, 'Chhurbura' who was considered to be the real hero of Mizo folktales must be the most interesting character in the world of Mizo Folktales. Chhurbura's humour is inexhaustible and it is interesting for everybody. He may be considered as the most memorable hero in the world of simpleton. His simplicity and ignorance about the thing he takes up and his stupid way of life makes everyone happy and laugh. He is the subject of laughter. In the tale of 'Chhurbura and Chengkek', 'Chhura and the Banyan Tree' we find the extreme simplicity of 'Chhurbura' the hero of this two tales. The name Chhurbura signifies that he himself is an idiot. In the tale of 'Chhurbura and Chengkek', we find the inability of Chhura to pick up the fruit of Chengkek due to his ignorance and foolishness whereas the branch of the Chengkek falls near to him, instead of picking up the fruits of Chengkek he simply said that if Nahaia is here with me, he will be easily picked up the fruits of Chengkek by bending the branch of Chengkek which is within the reach of Chhura that produced incessant laughter to everyone. The same thing happened to the tale of 'Chhura and Banyan Tree' which produced more laughter. His parent told Chhura to start cooking when the ray of the setting sun falls on the branch of the Banyan tree. It may be due to lack of understanding or due to ignorance Chhura climbed the tree of Banyan carrying all of cooking pots and utensils to cook on the branch of Banyan Tree. It is indeed quite troublesome for him to climb the tree with all utensils and pot for cooking which produced inner joy and non-stop laughter to everyone who reads the tale of Chhurbura. By reading the tale of 'Chhura and Chengkek' we can well perceive that those who have no sense of self-reliance and confidence can never expect the fruits of success. Rather must we make it a point to tackle every problem that comes before us. By reading every folklore or folktale of Mizo, everyone will find morality and sensibility and they will surely enjoy reading it. Some folklores of Mizo like 'How the Mushroom Started', 'Monkey and Bear', 'Chawngmawii and Hrangchhuana', and so many others have sensational appeal and convey moral lesson to all the readers. By reading the story of 'How the Mushroom Started', we are forced to love our parents and we know that we should be careful not to do anything wrong which might bring unhappiness to us. The words below have a sensational appeal to us.

> Swallow me up, O strong clay mound,
> My little sister no cucumber can give
> Swallow me up, O strong clay mound.

By reading this we feel pity for the elder who does not have even a single cucumber.

Besides folktales Mizos have folk/traditional songs like—Chawngchen Zai, Chai hla, Bawh hla, Hlado, Chheih Zai, Tlanglam Zai, Ralrun Zai. It is quite clear that even our forefathers expressed their rustic feelings with simple diction which became the songs of the particular group of folk. It is a fact that Mizo folk songs are of different types and of different styles composed by different persons on different subjects. We have to note that in some of the Mizo folk songs, the name of the composer or name of the tune/flow of songs can be identified. This is in fact, one point of its uniqueness for the readers of Mizo folk songs. Love is the principal theme of the Mizo folk songs.

A systematic study of Mizo folk songs leads us to understand the status of women in the society of Mizos. It is clear that without a sense of individuality, a sense of tragedy and liberty, these folk songs will never come into existence. It is unique that women played a vital role at the time when Mizo folk songs were composed. One example from the work of these women folk has been shown here. When we read the story of Miss Laltheri, the youngest daughter of Chief Lalsavunga, who had fallen in love with a young man named Chalthanga, who was a poor commoner, we come to realize that she is the real portrait of a tragic figure as she is not allowed to marry such a poor commoner (Hnamchawm) being the daughter of a chief. When her brothers beheaded Chalthanga whom she loved dearly and whole-heartedly she lost her sense and expressed her grief, crying incessantly, she tore off her clothes and threw away all her lovely beads and lay down on the courtyard stripping off her clothes. Out of perplexity her mother asked her to wear her clothes and necklaces. But not heeding to her mother's behest Laltheri rigidly replied.

Mummy, I shall not wear my clothes
As my lover lies dead cold and deep down,

and with a feeling of grief and depression she further blamed her parents for their wrongful deeds of killing her lover against her will;

How thoughtless you are
My Mummy and Daddy,
Hanging the head of Chalthanga
On our Courtyard.

All these verses remind us of Shelley's statement in his "Defence of poetry". The freedom of women produced the poetry of sexual love. Love became a religion, the idols of whose worship were ever present.

There are some other folk songs which are not mentioned here. In fact, we find the uniqueness and richness in Mizo folk songs. Poetry had been serving as the common medium of expression of love among the Mizos. Saikuti (1842-1921), one of the most famous poetesses of the 19th century also contributed a great number of songs on the theme of Love. In one of her love songs Saikuti expressed her love for her sweetheart. A mizo young lover also expresss his deep feeling of love in the following lines:

How I wish, my sweetheart,
That we both be stars in the sky,
And let people say what they will.

It seems that during the primitive time our forefathers used to express their feeling of love by means of composing songs. The character of the traditional Mizo culture is reflected not only in its social institutions and folktales, but also in folk songs. The Mizos are justifiably well known as a "Singing Tribe". Its musical tradition, unlike those of some other tribes, were well developed even before the coming of Christianity and exposure to Western music. Besides these folk songs, love and the then contemporary songs are also composed by Mizo poets out of their experience which can be sung mostly with Guitar and Piano. Amongst numbers of poets I should not forget to mention the name of Rokunga, who is called (a poet of the century). He is a poet of the nature, regional poet. His love for nature and his description of nature is comprehensive and all-inclusive.

Most of the Mizos can sing any kind of songs and they loved group singing too. The Mizos have a cultural background abounding in songs, poems, folklore, dramas, novels and even cultural dances, all of which are very rich aesthetically, Mizo songs or poem include different kinds of songs like devotional, traditional, love, nature, contemporary and gospel songs. These songs are meaningful and touching to the hearer and singers. There are some famous and acclaimed poets among the Mizos—Among those poets I should not forget to mention the name of Rokunga (poet of the century). Rokunga's most important subject is his poetry is his love for Mizoram. His description of the scenery, the beauty, the people, their occupation, their laughter, hardship, the dreams that he build, the future that he visualize are all peculiar and confined to Mizoram and the beauty of Mizoram is immortalized through his vision. Rokunga presents the hilly and rugged features of Mizoram and transforms it into a paradise on earth. In one of his famous poems *"Kan zotlang ram nuam"* explains the beauty of Mizoram and says;

Kan zotlang ram nuam hi chhawrpial run i iange
Hallo ten lungruala dar ang kan lenna.
(Our beautiful hilly Zoram is like paradise
It's a peaceful land where we live together without enmity)

Rokunga engraves the beauty of Mizoram into the heart of the Mizos through his poem.

Hei aia ram nuam zawk hi awm chuangin ka ring nem maw.

(I don't think there is a place better and more pleasant than this.)

Rokunga says that it is nature that provides us with songs to sing and lines to write. In the second stanza of the poem *"Lei mawina thinlai ti hlimtu"*, the voice of nature, as heard by Rokunga, the poet come alive with all its beauty singing but like a melodious choir, playing their own part. He writes:

Tlang sang thing zar mawi leh phai zawla,
Suang lungpui leh luipui luang ri;
Vanrang chhum leh thlifim leng velin,
Khawvel mawi hi hlamawi an pe.
(The waving trees on hills, pleasant noise
Of rocks and the sound of the flowing rivers
The trailing cloud and the blowing breeze
Provide this world with a refreshing and wonderful song.)

There are some other poems in Mizo which is regarded as a romantic poetry. When we see the song of Hrawva a romantic poet, we feel that Mizo poetry approaches 'the romantic agony' of natural injustice

Dogs and goats lie in their dry shed,
Poor boy makes mother of the sow
Underneath the house. (Rairahtea Hla)
(*The song of poor orphan boy*)

Vankhama's love poetry reaches beyond the emotional dimension in the lover's altruism.

A glimpse of you brightens our hearts,
A slight on your name but turns it cold
The best of best I would for you.

Another song of Rokunga reflects the beauty of Mizoram and its people *'Ka pianna zoram nuam' (Our Homeland zoram calm)*

Hazy mist afloat a dark green forest,
Enfolding zoram our charming land;
Gazing round on lonely days and musing
More gorgeous, the land zo people roam.

The Mizo people became familiar to the Western musical instruments only by the twentieth century. The first Western musical instruments entering Mizoram were the mouth organ and the full Organ brought by a missionary's wife, Mrs. Fraser in 1907. But Dr. and Mrs. Fraser returned to England after a few years stay in Mizoram, and the local youth had no time to learn to play those instruments.

After a long recess of more than ten years, Mizo youth became acquainted with the modern musical instruments in 1925. Vankhama (1906-70) was one of the notable pioneers who cultivated the seed of the modern musical instruments in the heart of Mizo youth. Besides these songs, there are more wonderful devotional and Gospel songs. These kind of devotional songs penetrated deep into the heart of the people.

The song, which is composed by Liangkhaia (eminent historian, theologian, preacher and poet of Mizo), '*Wonderful sacrifice of Jesus Christ'*, the son of God for all of us. By reading the first stanza

1. Wondrous words which I can't express
Is the story of calvary
How is Jesus Christ, the only son of God
Crucified on the Mount of Calvary
For the sinners like me, he was crucified.

We are made to appreciate the value of Mt. Calvary. Another devotional song is *'For God so loved the world'* composed by Rokunga. This song tells us that God loves everyone and his mercy flows through every place.

1. For God so loved this world of us
That he had given his only son to us
Flows and swells through every place
For those who had a faith in him
Will get eternal bliss and life.

Most of Mizos are impressed by this kind of devotional and gospel songs. They are also impressed by the song of Nature too. Such beautiful song called *'To the wild cherry tree'* composed by Vankhama cherished the beautiful wild flower tree called *'Tlaizawng'* which is blooming in full when Christmas (the most important festival of Mizos) is coming near.

When Christmas comes to mark the Lord's birthday,
Tlaizawng begins to sprout and bloom;
....
I'll call you 'Fair Bloom' as your nickname;
.................non-fading flower:

This Tlaizawng flower attracts everyone and the writer of this poem also wished it to be bloom forever and not to fade away.

In fact, in the hearts of Mizo people, any kind of songs like songs in praise of natural beauty, and some romantic songs, love songs in praise of beautiful lady or folk songs are dear to most of the people. And after Christianity we Mizo people are impressed and easily influenced by the devotional or gospel songs. Actually, Mizos are fond of music. And in this modern, fast changing world we should get ready to wake up and challenge the world around us.

Here, I make conclusion with my own composed poem "Dauntless Spirit" with a spirit of inspiration and enthusiasm

Sometimes I confounded in this world,
Of illusion and fantasy where nothing is certain,
Still I am beckoned to strive and march forward,
To challenge every task and fight for my country.
Wake up from your sleep dear,
This is not a time to sleep and sit idle,
You are strongly insisted by your people,
To step and march forward with dauntless spirit.

Moreover, our Mizo literature is enriched by such an interesting novels and dramas which are written depicting Mizo life, society, customs, culture and tradition. Mizo dramas and novels portrayed the real characters, social life, culture and tradition of Mizo themselves that can be shown in another discussion.

WORKS CITED

English Poetry—Study Aid. 198. (Collection of Poems & Essays—Edited), 1986: 244, Aizawl: 1988.

Mizo Folklore-I: Folktales of Mizoram 218, (Hard Bound) Art & Culture, Mizoram and LTL Publications, Aizawl: 1997.

Mizo Songs and Folk Tales, Published by the National Sahitya Akademi, New Delhi, 2002 & 2009: 171.

Rokunga: *Thalaite Hla Bu*, 5th Edition, 2012, Gilzom Offset Press, Electrict Veng Aizawl.

Rokunga Memorial Committee: Rokunga Hlate, LV Art Chandmary, 2000.

Songs of Precious Blood 56 (PYF Christian Song book—Edited): 2000.

Thanmawia R.L., *Mizo Poetry*, Din Din Heaven, Ramhlun South, Aizawl, 1998.

Thanmawia R.L. *Tidamtu Rokunga*. Chuailo-I. Aizawl: Gilzom Offset. R.L. Thanmawia, 2006.

❑❑❑

A Study of the "*Bani*" of *Sant* Ravidas in the *Guru Granth Sahib* from a Bakhtinian Perspective

JASWINDER SINGH AND RANO RINGO

THE objective of this paper is to study the "*bani*" of *Sant* Ravidas in the *Guru Granth Sahib* as an example of "heteroglossia, multiple voices of a given culture, people and epoch" (*From the Prehistory of the Novelistic Discourse* 60) propounded by Mikhail Bakhtin in his seminal essays compiled in *The Dialogic Imagination: Four Essays by M.M. Bakhtin*. Heteroglossia, polyphony and dialogism are some of the key terms whereby Bakhtin postulates the concept of social discourse inherent in genres such as the novel wherein social conflicts and tensions are invariably underpinned (*Discourse in the Novel* 259). His theoretical judgments on the characteristics of social discourse can be extended to the Indian tradition and to those cultural works which can be viewed as a part of the larger social spectrum. To understand the cultural and social spectrum as whole, the interacting social voices in this social spectrum need to be analyzed and understood. The study contends that Mikhail Mikhailovich Bakhtin's notion of "social heteroglossia" (*Discourse in the Novel* 284) does not confine its modular application to the canonical Russian or European texts, rather its validity can be traced and tested in holy texts such as the *Guru Granth Sahib*. Further, Bakhtin while theorizing the dialogical philosophy has kept the European genres in mind but insofar as the *Bani*[1] is concerned it is different in character and background. The present paper attempts to foreground the dialogic relationship between *Sant* Ravidas' select compositions which are also a part of the *Guru Granth Sahib* and the wider cultural spectrum wherein they were composed which resulted in disagreement leading to liberation. The "*bani*"[2] of *Sant* Ravidas acts as one of the voices in his compositions which can be viewed as a dialogical voice or a double voiced discourse as propounded by Bakhtin. The Bakhtinian theoretical framework has been employed to study the internal dialogism for explicating the rich semantic base of the compositions; only those compositions have been studied which perfectly exemplify the "double voice" (Bakhtin,*Discourse in the Novel* 324) mechanism. The compositions selected as examples to illustrate the Bakhtinian dialogism have been extracted from the *Guru Granth Sahib*. The paper contends that the *bani* of *Sant* Ravidas is heteroglot. The paper also contends that despite the poetic form of the *bani* of *Sant* Ravidas, it remains inherently dialogical. In fact, the whole *Guru Granth Sahib* is in the form of verses and not written in the prose form. Although Bakhtin categorically rejects the possibility of active dialogism in any kind of poetry, this paper hopes to establish that dialogism is an integral part not only of the *bani* of *Sant* Ravidas, but of the *Guru Granth Sahib* as whole. The dialogical validity of the *bani* of *Sant* Ravidas can be proved only by establishing it as a social discourse with its all necessary heteroglot traits. The present study will demonstrate step by step that the *bani* of *Sant* Ravidas in particular and the whole *Bani* in general have precisely ingrained dialogical features despite *Bani*'s non-prose form. This is perhaps because the heteroglot forces which gave rise to the compositions in the *Guru Granth Sahib* were different from those that prevailed in Europe.

In contrast to the European tradition, the Indian tradition which had a long history of writing all type of literature had used verse as predominant vehicle of expressing ideas. The literary tradition in India had employed poetic form where language realized its full capacity to express idea fully (Gerow 252). "Kavya" as a form had been used in writing dictionaries, scientific or astronomical treatises and medical works (Winternitz 14) along with devotional and secular literature. Though the Indian style of writing religious and other secular works in verse form had persistently been the dominating tendency, yet the socio-historical conditions had not been ignored in the formation of such poetic tradition. Edwin Gerow characterizes the seminal function of "kavya" style in the Indian tradition:

> Kavya, though it is a kind of language different in itself is not seen apart from and indifferent to the social and intellectual dimension of language to society itself. (*Indian Poetics* 220)

Besides, the evolution of the Indian tradition into multiple traditions, cultures, languages and scriptures can be ascribed to the open and unfixed character of Indian socio-cultural tradition, though the hierarchical systems had made all attempts to curb or fix the voices of "others" or other traditions during the evolution of this diversity. The development of various traditions and diverse cultures had not only shaped and defined the history and culture of India, but it also became the dialogic center of different cultures. The development of new voices in the form of new religions, cultures and languages had cast a shadow on the authoritarian and hegemonic forces. The religious and philosophical variety of the Vedic and other traditions like Buddhist, Jainism, Saiva-Sidhanta, Vaisnava, Samkhya, Yoga, Nyaya, Advaita, can be viewed as different units of dialogic and argumentative tradition of Indian "heterodoxy" (Sen 21). In this Indian dialogic context the *Guru Granth Sahib* as a social discourse has not only continued the argumentative tradition of India, but also retained a central significance in shaping the medieval history of India. Thus, the study also aims to place the *Guru Granth Sahib* in the larger dialogic perspective through the voice of *Sant* Ravidas as his voice is integral to the whole *Guru Granth Sahib*. In fact the whole *Guru Granth Sahib* can be seen as one of the participating links in the chain of socio-cultural communication. The voice of *Sant* Ravidas can be assessed as one of the representative links of this widening and deepening social diversity. The *Guru Granth Sahib* or the poetic compositions of Guru Nanak, Kabir and Ravidas were dialogical even much before the beginning of Novel as social discourse. Such facts prompt us to believe that Indian tradition has survived its dialogic forces even under harsh authoritative regimes. Thus our study contends that nowhere poetic form of *Sant* Ravidas' utterance restrains heteroglossia to flourish itself. Before coming down to the utterance of *Sant* Ravidas in the *Guru Granth Sahib*, it is necessary to review Bakhtin's opinion on the constraints of heteroglossia in poetry.

Heteroglossia and Its Constraints in Poetry

Since the whole *Guru Granth Sahib* and the *bani* of *Sant* Ravidas were composed in poetic form, it is necessary to review Bakhtin's views on poetry as he himself rejects any scope of active heteroglossia in poetic genres. According to Bakhtin, Heteroglossia operates dominantly in all social discourses and novelistic discourse is a rich "soil" (*Discourse in the Novel* 325) to cultivate heteroglossia. But Bakhtin precisely denies and rejects any scope of heteroglossia in poetry. He claims that the heteroglot forces remain passive in both high and low form of poetry (*Discourse in the Novel* 296 and 333). The primary reasons of its passivity are its absence from the zone of "contact" (Bakhtin, *Epic and Novel* 35) and its aesthetic imagination based on "memory" (Bakhtin, *Epic and Novel* 18-19). According to Bakhtin, the linguistic world of poetry is unitary and poetry unlike novel eliminates all "seeds" of different "worldviews" which are the elementary features of novel. It has no concrete elements of other "professional jargons", "tendencies" and "directions" (*Discourse in the Novel* 297). The context in a poem functions merely as semantic unity and remains a unitary language system. Bakhtin further claims that a poem does not show any particular "speech manner" and "socially typically linguistic face" which create a distinct "personality" (*Discourse in the Novel* 297). Hence, it lacks a linguistic direction and moves freely in its own world and ideological sphere. Speaking on the characteristics of epic poetry, he analyzes it as a genre of distant zone which is far away from the contemporary themes teeming with personal experience and social worldviews (*Epic and Novel* 13). He claims that the high genre of epic poetry is based on "memory" and "national tradition" (*Epic and Novel* 13-15), which takes it away from the territory of everyday language and contemporary world of reality. Epic, according to him, is a genre where the author and its readers are situated at the plane of absolute past (*Epic and Novel* 13). This is the time of national foundation of cultures or traditions (*Epic and Novel* 15).

Thus, our understanding of Bakhtinian notions on heteroglossia validates that none of the Bakhtinian parameters negate and restrict the presence of heteroglot forces in the poetic compositions of *Sant* Ravidas. His *bani* is a product of his spiritual wisdom and practical "knowledge" (Bakhtin, *Epic and Novel* 15) of social reality. The *bani* of *Sant* Ravidas provides a glimpse of his contemporary world and his keen observation of day-to-day practical affairs. Even the whole *Guru Granth Sahib* in general becomes a platform for the Gurus and *Sants* to convey their spiritual and empirical knowledge of religious and social life. The voice of *Sant* Ravidas in the *Guru Granth Sahib* as a social discourse records the social and theological conflicts of its time. As a participant in the ongoing social dialogue of its epoch, the voice of *Sant* Ravidas manifests a phenomenon of "event interrelationship" (Bakhtin, *PDP* 9). As a social discourse it provides space to the events juxtaposed contrapuntally and manifests the "reigning" (Bakhtin, *PDP* 90) and non-reigning social voices of the time. These voices manifest the social situations of its time. The voice of *Sant* Ravidas in the *Guru Granth Sahib* manifests this social reality by engaging in a social dialogue with other "reigning voices" (Bakhtin, *PDP* 90) of the time (Hindu sectarian forces). It becomes a distinct voice and separate belief-system when it redefines and reformulates the object or idea which were already defined and described by other pre-existing socio-ideological systems. This encounter with other socio-ideological systems results in dialogical interaction.

To visualize this dialogic encountering of socio-ideological systems, the concept and categories of "social heteroglossia" (*Discourse in the Novel* 284) have to be examined in the compositions of *Sant* Ravidas in the *Guru Granth Sahib*. To locate and validate the forces of social heteroglossia, the paper will study the hymns of *Sant* Ravidas from Bakhtinian concept of "utterance" and "rejoinder" (*The Problem of Speech Genre* 71). Bakhtin predominantly uses the term "utterance" (*Discourse in the Novel* 271) to cover all kinds of written texts and speech acts as communicative units of socio-cultural environment in an epoch. All such forms of "utterance" (Bakhtin, *Discourse in the Novel* 271) are social in character and dialogic in nature. Bakhtin affirms their dialogic indispensability:

> Any utterance—from a short (single word) rejoinder in everyday dialogue to the large novel or scientific treatise—has, so to speak, an absolute beginning and an absolute end; its beginning is preceded by the utterances of others, and its end is followed by the responsive utterances of others. (*The Problem of Speech Genre* 71)

Explaining the socio-ideological network of utterance, Bakhtin identifies an utterance as a unit of larger speech communication which through its social voice is related to other utterances to which it responds and those which respond to it like any rejoinder as in an ordinary process of dialogue or conversation (Bakhtin, *The Problem of Speech Genre* 76). An utterance not only satisfies its semantic requirements but also fulfills its heteroglot requirements as a "rejoinder" (*Discourse in the Novel* 272-77). All utterances inhere the force of "rejoinder" (*Discourse in the Novel* 276-77). Rejoinder as an utterance carries the context of its own as well as the context of the other preceding or coexisting utterances. Bakhtin's notion of utterance as rejoinder befits the *bani* of *Sant* Ravidas. As a rejoinder the *bani* of *Sant* Ravidas responds not only to the coexisting ideologies but also addresses the established preexisting ideologies (ideological systems). Any utterance functioning as rejoinder acts as a double voice discourse or speech (Bakhtin, *Discourse in the Novel* 276-77). Explaining the double voiced characteristic of a social utterance, Bakhtin defines it as a constitution of two voices, accents, languages, worldviews or points of views which are artistically or intentionally stratified (*Discourse in the Novel* 360).

Bakhtin goes further in explaining the role of language in nurturing and fertilizing such multiple voices, languages, accents and points of view in his long and theoretical essays compiled in *The Dialogic Imagination.* These long essays frame a comprehensive theory on the generic development of Novel as a social utterance which is markedly pregnant with multiple voices. According to him a language is not a unitary system (*Discourse in the Novel* 288). It is socially plural, open and heteroglot. Language as a living entity or phenomenon is surrounded by concrete social-ideological belief systems (*Discourse in the Novel* 288). As a phenomenon, language is a process of "historical becoming" (Bakhtin, *Discourse in the Novel* 288). Here historical becoming stands for language's widening and ever growing social space or domain. The features of social phenomenon and "historical becoming" (Bakhtin, *Discourse in the Novel* 288) fill language in utterances with multiple worldviews and varied social-ideological systems. These ideological systems or utterances in an epoch (in past and future also) work as elements of language which contain "semantic" or "axiological" values (Bakhtin, *Discourse in the Novel* 288). These elements are not only dialectological in nature, but also behave dialogically when set against one another. Language is a constantly widening system where its elements have not only got space, but also a background to start dialogue. Thus, Bakhtin's cogent claim of coexisting voices representing varied socio-ideological "belief systems" (*Discourse in the Novel* 288) can be examined in the language of *Sant* Ravidas in the *Guru Granth Sahib* and his concept of "utterance" can be fittingly employed to illustrate the "socio-linguistic speech diversity and multilanguagedness" (*Discourse in the Novel* 325-26) in *Sant* Ravidas' voice.

This constant widening and deepening "historical becoming" (Bakhtin, *Discourse in the Novel* 288) phenomenon of language prompts Bakhtin to declare the unfinalizibility of idea or subject. Bakhtin postulates that new utterances establish dialogue with other utterances and retain all potential to anticipate response from the future. This constant growth of utterance does not allow idea to be completely exhausted (*PDP* 87-88). He claims that idea/subject is a process of "psychological evolution" (*PDP* 88). Idea, according to him, never gets exhausted, it never dies; moreover, it develops, takes shape, finds new verbal expressions, gives birth to new ideas, and enters into new dialogic relationship at every stage (*PDP* 87-88). Bakhtin claims that idea/subject is not an authoritative domain or "permanent resident rights" of someone (*PDP* 88). It cannot

not grow in single consciousness. The idea like social reality is future oriented and still, so much is left to be written or spoken about it. Such unfinalized and openended characteristics of dialogue predispose Bakhtin to conclude that all languages, dialects, texts and cultures are unfixed and open to more thoughts, views and expressions and transformations. The compositions of *Sant* Ravidas in the *Guru Granth Sahib* perfectly epitomize Bakhtin's notion of unfinalizibility of idea when *Sant* Ravidas himself sets free the idea/subject (God, worship, prayer, social hierarchy, etc.) from the reigning authoritative brahmanic voice and brings it to the public zone. His voice on social and religious events partakes into the socio-cultural communication as a participant. His point of view on social and religious motifs significantly reevaluates the concept of God and society whose earlier interpretations and values were authoritative privilege of hegemonic forces. His voice sets free the concept/subject (God and society) from the closed system and brings into the open system through reformulation and reinterpretation of it.

Guru Granth Sahib as Rejoinder

Though the present paper has confined its study to the writings of *Sant* Ravidas in the *Guru Granth Sahib*, yet the heteroglot background and forces of the *Guru Granth Sahib* as a whole cannot be ignored as it integrally incorporates the consciousness of *Sant* Ravidas.[3] It is necessary to talk about the general heteroglot forces of the whole*Guru Granth Sahib* as it will consolidate our contention that the dialogic forces are inherent features of *Sant* Ravidas' voice as it conspicuously represents the voice of the whole *Guru Granth Sahib*. The whole *Guru Granth Sahib* as a social discourse precisely manifests all the conditions and qualification necessary for "social heteroglossia" (Bakhtin, *Discourse in the Novel* 284). The very external structure of the *Guru Granth Sahib* makes it a multi-voiced structure. The whole *Guru Granth Sahib* is a compiled work of Six Gurus and *Sants*/poetic scholars. The *Guru Granth Sahib* as a religious scripture sets a unique example by incorporating the voices of Muslim and Hindu *Sant*s along with the Sikh Gurus. Apart from the Hindu and Muslim voices, the *Guru Granth Sahib* also affords space to the marginal voices to project their consciousness. This incorporation of the compositions from different sects and sections was done at the time when social divisions and discrimination were at its peak. *Bani* (the *Guru Granth Sahib*) had come forward to unfold wisdom and enlighten the ordinary people who were trapped in the darkness of rituals, idolatry, social hierarchy, superstitions (Daljeet Singh 168-73) and polytheism. As the social atrocities and religious misguidance had fastened its roots deep and had been accelerating considerably, the religious and social revolution had become the need which materialized in the teachings of the Sikh Gurus and other *Sant*s. *Bani* made all efforts to make people aware of social reality and some false practices. Hence, a notion of opposition and disagreement had evolved against the contemporary practices ingrained in the Hindu sectarian discourses (Daljeet Singh 155) which had taken their shape from the authoritative preexisting and coexisting Hindu discourses. To spread this wave of reform, a voice was needed and hence, *Bani* came as a voice against another's "voice" (Bakhtin, *Discourse in the Novel* 348) or as a new accent of distinct social and religious ideology.

Apart from its revolting character, it served the basic religious and social needs of common people. The voice of the Guru became a new voice, a new language and a new social-ideological identity. The basic tenets of *Guru Granth Sahib* were to "re accentuate" (Bakhtin, *Discourse in the Novel* 421) and refill the notions of God, worship, social and moral obligations, intending productive correction. The "belief-system" of the *Guru Granth Sahib* was entirely distinct in ideological character to its (Hindu sectarian philosophies) counterpart(s). Hence the *Guru Granth Sahib* itself entered the dialogic relationship of contest and contradiction. This was the relationship of dissonance and dismissal of old definitions of the object (God, worship, prayer, social and moral obligation including social hierarchy). From Bakhtinian perspective, the *Bani* too orients towards its "apperceptive background" (*Discourse in the Novel* 282) where while dialogizing with other (Hindu) voices it "reaccentuates" (Bakhtin, *Discourse in the Novel* 421) and reprocesses the subject like God, worship, rituals, liturgy and other social values differently. During the course of this "reaccentuation" (Bakhtin, *Discourse in the Novel* 421) and redefinition, it interacts with another consciousness. Since the basic purpose of the *Bani* is to guide a common man,[4] it had to use the common object (theme) and concepts to show a distinct "belief-system". The *Bani* responds as a rejoinder in order to redefine and re accent the object (God and other earthly matters). To reflect the reality and social truth, the *Bani* had to be a participant through this common contextual background to respond to the other "belief-systems" (Bakhtin, *Discourse in the Novel* 304). The other belief systems cannot be contacted without being indulged in the social dialogue. The *Bani* was not meant for the contemporary generation only, but it orients to the past and to the future (social discourse). *Bani* as rejoinder becomes a reformative and enlightening step which attempts to displace the discourses based on "ritualism and formalism" (Daljeet Singh 70). Thus, the "apperceptive background" (Bakhtin, *Discourse in the Novel* 282) here provides the common conceptual level at which two different social and religious ideologies interact or "fight" (Bakhtin, *Discourse in the Novel* 360).

Sant Ravidas: Historical Background of His Compositions

There are 41 hymns of *Sant* Ravidas which were included in the *Guru Granth Sahib*. These 41 hymns of *Sant* Ravidas were incorporated in the *Guru Granth Sahib* by Guru Arjan Dev, the fifth Guru of the Sikh. As the compositions of *Sant* Ravidas matched and agreed with the socio-religious ideology of the *Guru Granth Sahib*, Guru Arjan Dev had incorporated select compositions (hymns) at the beginning of the seventeenth century (1604 AD). *Sant* Ravidas was born during the *bhakti* period in the medieval age in India when there was a decline in the social and religious order. The *bhakti* period is also known as the age of spiritual revolt (Chatterjee 11) and mysticism. Kabir, who was also the contemporary of *Sant* Ravidas, himself openly, criticized the ritualistic and formalistic ways of devotion and other social practices. This was the period when various Hindu sects had emerged across India and the north had become the hub of this *bhakti* period. *Sant* Ravidas was a mystic who had attained a spiritual experience on the basis of his unflinching devotion and love towards God. He was well familiar with social tensions and discrimination of his times, as he himself was born to a low caste family and had to face the brunt of Brahmanic autocracy and persecution. Like Kabir, he devotedly attained a spiritual wisdom that motivated his intuition and soul to voice the actual character of God[5] and also confront the sham social hierarchy through his writing. His voice was a revolt against the ritualistic worship, idolatry system and arbitrary social hierarchy. It is crystal clear that a revolt in the form of compositions cannot take place without its causal forces. A revolt needs a background (context) and cause (socio-ideological theories of caste formation). Thus, the *bani* of *Sant* Ravidas partakes in the socio-cultural dialogue with the contemporary and pre-existing belief systems.

The "revolt" (Chatterjee 11) does not imply any militaristic movement of mystics in this medieval period. It was an ideological revolt. This revolt was to "de scribe" (Gurbhagat Singh 4) a belief-system of idolatry and ritualism. Many scholars point out about this revolt in the mystical age of medieval India. M.A. Macauliffe traces the reason of this revolt in the following words:

> There have lived in India from time immemorial Sants and thinkers who were dissatisfied with the superstitions and religious vagaries of the Hindus. They gradually evolved a belief in one God and preceded Guru Nanak as the dawn before the sunrise. (1)

Another Sikh scholar Daljeet Singh compares these two ideologies by naming them as "Activity bhakti" and "Quietist bhakti" (Daljeet Singh 177). He calls the *Bani* a part of the activity bhakti that advocates morally rich and active social life. Quietist bhakti, on the other hand, advocates a departure from social and moral obligations of life and promotes salvation at personal level by shunning social duties. The other ritualistic and social laws were almost as same as they were defined and prescribed in Vedas and Upanishads. One of the active measures of this Activist bhakti was to hew out caste system. It became evident when Guru Arjan Dev himself gave an equal space to the *bani* of low caste *Sant*s among the compositions of the high caste Gurus. Daljeet Singh also points out the growing critical and reproaching attitude between these two different movements. They were critical of each other. This critical relationship provides heteroglot space to interacting ideological positions. Without this critical interaction, the *bani* of *Sant* Ravidas would have been monologic. This critical interrelationship helped in sprouting heteroglot elements. Daljeet Singh notices this space of ideological conflict:

> The two systems of bhakti, Activity bhakti and Quietist bhakti, are independent and different. There is a tendency among scholars trained in Quietist traditions to criticize the Activist religions and even to consider the activist tendencies to be degenerate or a fall. On the other hand, scholars from the Activist systems are equally critical of the Quietist systems which even they call of escapist and deficient (*Essentials of Sikhism* 177)

So it is understood that the uprising was ideological in character and relativized in direction. The compositions of *Sant* Ravidas were a form of "revolt" (Chatterjee 11) and his language of revolt has all characters of Bakhtinian "rejoinder". Michael Holoquist calls such forms of interaction as "the two fundamentals of all communication" (xix).

Thus, the *bani* of *Sant* Ravidas can be viewed as a revolting dialogic utterance which significantly manifests all features of Bakhtinian "rejoinder" (Bakhtin, *Discourse in the Novel* 276-77). His voice intentionally uses the "images" and accents (Bakhtin, *DI* 356) of other ideological voice(s) which get activated at the conceptual axis where *Sant* Ravidas "re accentuates" (Bakhtin, *Discourse in the Novel* 421) the object already "charged" (Bakhtin, *Discourse in the Novel* 276) with the preexisting and coexisting ideological belief systems. These "images" (Bakhtin, *DI* 356) become "the object of representation" (Bakhtin, *Discourse in the Novel* 312) in the *bani* of *Sant* Ravidas. Through this object of representation, an interaction between two ideological systems at the conceptual level is conspicuous. The use of these images was intentional and directional. The objective to employ these images was to foreground the social reality. Thus, the interaction results in opposition and ideological conflict which establishes the voice of *Sant* Ravidas as a distinct self-conscious voice. Daljeet Singh confirms the conflicting interaction of these two religious forces:

> The radical bhagats not only disregarded all that but ridiculed it. In fact, they attacked Vaisanvism and Vaisnava Bhakti as a whole. Evidently, the two systems are so much apart and, even opposed to each other, that there is hardly a meeting ground between them. (*The Sikh Ideology*, 109-10)

Thus, it is clear that the *Bani* in general and the compositions of *Sant* Ravidas in particular, are socially conscious in message, tone and context. It is entirely teeming with social and religious ideology. Its content, philosophy, style and language all lead it to the realm of contemporary world of reality which is based on personal and spiritual experience. It is not a discourse which points its events connected to an imagined past. It lives in the zone of "present" (Bakhtin, *Epic and Novel* 30) which is a zone of "contact" (Bakhtin, *Epic and Novel* 31). An ordinary reader of *bani* can view it, takes it into personal experience, analyze it, can interpret from his point of view or situation (Pashaura Singh 260-61). Thus, it does not show any severe rigidity of an authoritative text. *Bani* is not contextually neutral. As far as the *bani* of *Sant* Ravidas is concerned, it does not let the other "words" (Bakhtin, *Discourse in the Novel* 298) die. It keeps them alive to continue the dialogic relationship. *Sant*'s *bani* does not let itself turn into an abstract context. The voice of *Sant* supplies "soil" (Bakhtin, *Discourse in the Novel* 325) to the other ideological "consciousness" (Bakhtin, *Discourse in the Novel* 359) to grow which subsequently results in opposition and disagreement. Without letting other ideology existing at the conceptual plane, the voice of *Sant* will sound abstract and monologic.

Such ideological opposition and conflict could be conspicuous, according to Bakhtin, only in "low prosaic language" of novelistic discourse (*From the Prehistory of Novelistic Discourse* 75). The terms "low prosaic language" and "conversational language" (Bakhtin, *From the Prehistory of Novelistic Discourse* 75) do not imply any notion of degradation or disrepute. Rather this low language is a normal and ordinary language—a language of "everyday life" (Bakhtin, *Discourse in the Novel* 331) which is generally a language of conversation. This everyday or ordinary language is a fundamental part of novelistic discourse. The finest character of this language is its authenticity and its proximity with "zone" of "contact" (Bakhtin *Epic and Novel* 31). It is a real language with concrete dialectological mixture. This notion of ordinary language is convincingly available in the *Guru Granth Sahib* in general and in the utterance of *Sant* Ravidas in particular. *Bani* is based on the spiritual experience of the Gurus and other mystics and the language serves all its purpose with simple tone of ordinary semantics and syntax. It is an address to the common folk. This linguistic characteristic of *Bani* is confirmed by many Sikh scholars and thinkers. Surinder Singh Kohli, a scholar on the Adi Granth, comments on the character of the language used in the *Guru Granth Sahib*:

> Being folk poets, they spoke in that language which was understood by the masses.... Guru Nanak and Guru Arjan wrote in Sahaskriti also in order to convey their thoughts to these people. (45)

Thus, it can be stated that *Bani* is not a work of mere literary imagination. It is neither unitary nor abstract (context). It is proximate to a zone of contemporary reality. It retains a distinct social identity by having a distinct belief-system. The language is a simple language of everyday—*Santbhasha* (language of *Sant*s; Kalsi 36). So the possibility of a heterglot world considerably increases in the compositions of *Sant* Ravidas whose *bani* is the integral part of the whole *Guru Granth Sahib*.

Heteroglossia in the *bani* of *Sant* Ravidas

The dialogic mechanism in the *bani* of *Sant* Ravidas appears at the thematic and syntactic plane which ingrains the linguistic images of others' consciousness(s). *Sant*'s language holds two socio-ideological belief systems together through the images of "represented" and "representing" languages (Bakhtin, *Discourse in the Novel* 364). The other interacting language is not virtually apparent as it does not come upon at surface. This "another language" (Bakhtin, *Discourse in the Novel* 358) is inherent in the primary ideological utterance of the *Sant*. The two languages become concrete images of two distinct ideologies interacting at the conceptual space. The two different languages (voices) materialize concretely through the object representation. These languages (consciousnesses) hold a dialogic relationship through consistent "encounter" (Bakhtin, *Discourse in the Novel* 276). The dialogic encounter finally results into contradictions and disagreement. This dialogic relationship is a struggle to "liberate" (Bakhtin, *Discourse in the Novel* 348) an ideology from the rigidity of authoritative ideologies. Here the authoritative ideologies can be understood as reference to the dominant worldviews of "reigning" (Bakhtin, *PDP* 90) Hindu discourses. The axis at which this dissonance takes place is the common object which here the *bani* of *Sant* Ravidas is "representing" (Bakhtin, *Discourse in the Novel* 364). This object is already filled with Hindu ideological content (their notion on God, worship, prayer, social hierarchy and so forth) that is contradictory to the philosophical character of *Sant*'s *Bani*. The conceptual space of both the "consciousnesses" (Bakhtin, *Discourse in the Novel* 359-60) is relative. This concept or the object itself retains all points of disputes and contest which are socio-ideological (Bakhtin, *Discourse in the Novel* 276).

The voice of *Sant* Ravidas is charged with the ironic and parodic tones to drill the social reality. The basic objective behind using this style is to set a dialogue with other ideological position(s) which is based on "ritualism" (Daljeet Singh 70) and polytheism. The use of irony and humor has been made to correct and show the productive consciousness. It is not like a crude satirical contempt, but a dignified and enlightening voice emerges at the back of these ironic structures. The use of ironic and parodic discourse activates the dialogic interaction between two ideologies and one of them shows an ideological disagreement over the other. Bakhtin calls such mixing of two ideologies within a consciousness "intentional semantic hybrids" (*Discourse in the Novel* 360). The images in the form of names and practices (materials) are apparently a "represented consciousness" (Bakhtin, *Discourse in the Novel* 359) which have not been used merely as a syntactic necessity.

The direct use of the "image" (Bakhtin, *Discorse in the Novel* 358) of entities (Vedas and Puranas) and materials as prescribed in the Hindu scriptures, not only creates a space where two "socio-ideological"

(Bakhtin, *Discourse in the Novel* 276) consciousnesses can interact, but these images which carry their distinct ideological systems also become source of irony:

> In the Sat age was truth, in the Treta sacrifice, and in
> the Dwapar the performance of worship.
> In the three ages these three observances were established,
> but in the Kal age the Name is the only support.
> How shall I be saved?
> No one explaineth to me
> How my transmigration may cease.
> There are many forms of religion described, but every
> one appeareth to adopt his own.
> What are those acts by which I may be saved, and by
> the performance of which I may obtain all things?
> If what are merits and what demerits be decided by
> listening to the Veds and Purans, doubt shall result;
> Doubt shall thus ever dwell in the heart; who shall dispel pride?
>
> (M.A. Macauliffe[6] Vol. 6: 323)

This hymn of *Sant* Ravidas is incorporated in the Raag Gauri in the *Guru Granth Sahib*. The tone of *Sant* is critical and questioning. This is an argumentative voice. He is already informed about the preexisting situations of other times ("the Sat age was truth, in the Treta sacrifice, and in the Dwapar the performance of worship") from the early sources. He comes to know about these situations from "many forms of religions" who claimed to be original source for addressing spiritual "doubt". So they were the "utterance" of other "religions" who had proclaimed such knowledge of other times. Here the object is spiritual relief or personal salvation. The "Veds and Purans" had already filled this object with their "point of view" which becomes a point of disagreement as *Sant* himself does not find any solution at personal level. The solution to his spiritual dilemma lies in the "Naam". *Sant* is only repeating the words of other discourses which had offered their distinct solutions for spiritual dilemmas, yet he was dissatisfied with their voice. The recontextualization of the already spoken, creates a sense of "parodic stylization" (Bakhtin, *Discourse in the Novel* 364). The irony comes into picture when *Sant* exposes by saying that no authority properly knows the "reality" because these many forms of religions "appeareth to adopt his own". He creates the images of "Veds and Purans". These images are created neither to fill any syntactic or semantic purpose nor to produce aesthetic taste. These images carry their entire belief-systems in them. Moreover, the superficial reading can well interpret that they are used here to convey the inherent irony. Whereas, these sources were highly believed for its prophetic views, *Sant* finds its insufficiency and limitations in resolving his spiritual dilemma. The "Veds and Purans" were considered highly sufficient in addressing man's social and spiritual needs, but ironically, it could not "dispel" doubt of *Sant* Ravidas. Here two images appear which interact ideologically. Thus, the two worldviews on a single object (here it is salvation) come through a single utterance. The hymn being a single language is carrying two different ideologies (languages) which finally results into disagreement. This disagreement is evident in the voice of *Sant*. His belief (in the "kal age the Name is the only support") is a point of disagreement with "many forms of religions". The two points of view contradict on the ideological sphere.

Similar example of internal dialogism can be traced in his reference to his caste. *Sant* repeatedly mentions his low caste background. Two meanings can be taken as granted. The primary meaning conveys that he was in fact born in a humble and low background; second, he is distancing himself from the arbitrary social hierarchy which is a fabricated system of men. Hence, he believes, mystically, in two castes only—that is God and man. But, apart from this spiritual message of casteless character of man, the linguistic repetition of his humble background not only derides the makers of this system, but also recreates the image of the existing (brahmanic) voice of caste system. Significantly, *Sant* frequently recalls his caste by calling himself "tanner" repeatedly. This linguistic repetition is in fact the words of the existing belief-system (Vedic and other Hindu scriptures which define caste formation in society). His repetition seems purposely re-invoking of their system of caste formation. It can be understood as an ironic use of the words which he or his belief-system had never framed and by which *Sant* had to suffer throughout his life. This repetition is a "re accentuation" (Bakhtin, *Discourse in the Novel* 421) of what the Brahmanic system had used to call him, but here *Sant*'s repeated "re accentuation" (Bakhtin, *Discourse in the Novel* 421) disapproves any such categorization of humans. Thus, his style invokes a hidden ideology approving caste through his voice. The following is the part of his hymn incorporated in Raag Sorath:[7]

My caste is low, my lineage low, and base is my birth:
I have sought Thy shelter, O God, saith the tanner Ravidas.
(M.A. Macauliffe Vol. 6: 326)

Sant Ravidas frequently uses the word "*chamaar*"[8] (tanner) for himself. The word carries the ironic tone of the speaker. The word not only projects the "consciousness" (Bakhtin, *Discourse in the Novel* 276) of the caste-makers, but it also "refracts" (Bakhtin and Voloshinov, *The Formal Method in Literary Scholarship* extract in *The Bakhtin Reader* 128) the intention of *Sant* Ravidas who disapproves such assertions. Thus, it reflects a double voiced structure of the above couplet. This seems a kind of self-stigmatizing approach. But it is mocking in tone and at the conceptual level he is displacing any such categorization on the basis of caste. *Sant* Ravidas is reaccentuating the same words which he had to struggle with throughout his life. His words are the parodic use of the Brahmanic definitions of social hierarchy which contains all roots of inequality among men. The repetition produces an image of brahmanic instructions which formed the classes based on caste. But, from larger perspective this self-stigmatizing notion (revolt) is decentering such ideology of caste system. Thus, the two "socio-linguistic consciousnesses" (Bakhtin, *Discouse in the Novel* 360) can be understood from the parodic style of *Sant*.

Another example of the "double voiced" (Bakhtin, *Discourse in the Novel* 324) mechanism can be noticed in another hymn which is used as an *Aarti* (Sikh prayer) in the Sikh temples. This hymn is incorporated in Raag Dhanasari in the *Guru Granth Sahib*. The message of this hymn is simple and easily comprehensible from the hymn. The *Aarti* carries simple message of true love and devotion to God. *Sant* is preaching that an honest and pure heart is enough to worship the Almighty. There is no further need of any earthly materials and rituals to worship God. One's true love and devotion are the true materials to offer and rituals to perform. In the hymn he recounts various materials and rituals which are used in a formal Hindu worship. *Sant* Ravidas substitutes all these materials and rituals with his devotional remembrance of God:

Thy name, God, is mine Aarti and mine ablutions:
Without the name of God all display is vain.
Thy name is my prayer-mat, Thy name my saffron grater,
Thy name the saffron which I sprinkle for Thee;
Thy name is the water, Thy name the sandal, the repetition of

Thy name the grating thereof; taking it I offer it unto Thee;
Thy name is the lamp, Thy name the wick,
Thy name the oil I pour therein;
Thy name is the light which I have applied to it, and
which hath enlightened the whole world;
Thy name is the string, Thy name the necklace of flowers;
all the eighteen loads of vegetables are too impure to offer Thee.
Why should I offer Thee the work of Thy hands?
Thy name is the chauri which I wave over Thee.
The whole world is engrossed in the eighteen Purans, the
sixty-eight places of pilgrimage, and the four sources of life.
Saith Rav Das, Thy name is the Arati;
the true Name is the food I offer unto Thee, O God.

(M.A. Macauliffe Vol. 6: 333)

It can be noted from the above quoted hymn of *Sant* Ravidas that the images of two different ideologies are interacting at the surface level. The hymn shows two separate "socio-linguistic points of view" (Bakhtin, *Discourse in the Novel* 360) and the tone of opposition is also precisely evident. This hymn precisely reveals the conceptual plane of two interacting ideologies. These ideologies, as it is evident, are at odd and a sense of "agitation" is visible in the voice of *Sant*. The language is again stratified with ironic and parodic structures. *Sant* Ravidas is not recounting the names of these rituals and materials merely to describe a religion's way of worshipping. The notion behind creating such images of other ideological systems is to directly address the ruling voices (Vaudeville and Partin 193). His recounting of the ritualistic and formalistic method of prayer is intentional and based on his empirical experience of his time. He intentionally mentions or, speaking in Bakhtinian sense, is re accenting the prescribed norms to worship God as it is formally laid down in Hindu scriptures. The notion of "parodic stylization" (Bakhtin, *Discourse in the Novel* 364) surfaces when *Sant* "re accentuates" (Bakhtin, *Discourse in the Novel* 421) all the materials and rituals which are the indispensable part of Hindu form of prayer. In Hindu form of worshipping, these rituals and materials are not randomly or arbitrarily used. These are used according to the prescribed instructions by their authoritative scriptures. Again the parodic and ironic structures have been used to show the "limitations" and "insufficiency" (Bakhtin, *From the Prehistory of Novelistic Discourse* 56) of these methods of worshipping. The objective behind naming of all these different material and rituals is to convey the ironic overtones. The hymn creates the image of another's way of worshipping God to show its deficiency. His reference to such practices was to expose the inherent duplicity and insignificance. So the two different voices can be judged—a voice of *Sant* who finds this way of worshipping God is meaningless as this is "the work of Thy Hands?" and another voice (ideology) is the one which believes in this system of ritualism and formalistic way of worshipping God. The hymn also conveys a notion of role reversal—a dialogic assertion. It is a well-known fact that medieval period is also known as a period of restrictions and rigid observation of caste professions. During those times, even reciting a prayer by any low caste or *shudra* was strongly forbidden. The old scriptures and their subsequent forms had strongly divided the society (Daljeet Singh 120-21) according to different castes and their respective professions. The low castes were strongly forbidden to enter temples and offer prayers. It becomes a matter of surprise and courage as *Sant* Ravidas, for being a low caste, not only teaches natural way to cherish God, but also conveys his stern disagreement with the ritualistic and idolatory way of worshipping God. A low caste *Sant* is teaching a right method of paying "ablutions". A low caste *Sant* attempts to correct what is pointless or meaningless. This reversing of role reflects the ground figure dialogic metaphor where the dialogue between center and margin continues and no one takes a privilege position. Hence it can be generalized that the language of this hymn is "dialogically saturated" (Bakhtin, *Discourse in the Novel* 271).

Before arriving at the conclusion it can be stated that *Sant*'s voice not only stands against the existing voice of the ruling systems, but also becomes the "mirror of society" (Giri 79) by being a language of common people. The language of the whole *Bani* is not any official language or a language of the court; rather it became, unlike the official and ornamented languages of the court, the language of common man. The language of *Sant* becomes a voice that carries people's "aspirations" and "suffering" (Giri 83). *Sant*'s voice, as it belongs to the low class, turns out to be a voice of "courage" (Giri 84) when *Sant* speaks in a simple and ordinary language of the common people. The ordinary and unornamented language and style make the voice of *Sant* Ravidas a literature of public sphere where it is dialogically addressing to the other existing voices. His voice is a voice of confrontation against the Brahmanic logic and, moreover, the writing of *Sant* becomes a literature of affirmation of the self and a new consciousness. The common style and language not only put the voice of *Sant* into a direct dialogue with ruling belief-system, but also it dialogues with the common people who had the same pangs and dilemma.

Conclusion

It can be argued that *Sant*'s *bani* intentionally stratifies voices to redefine and disinfect reality from social discrimination and darkness. These voices interact at ideological level which is significantly inherent in the object reevaluation. The representation of the images of other's consciousness is to convey a rational understanding of the object. Though the compositions of *Sant* Ravidas are in poetic form, yet it satisfies all parameters of heteroglot framework. Its "ideologically saturated" (Bakhtin, *Discourse in the Novel* 271) heteroglot world distances it from being the closed monologic utterance. Thus, *Bani* as a social discourse carries a "concrete socio-linguistic belief-system that defines a distinct identity" (Bakhtin, *Discourse in the Novel* 356). Though the present analytical study is confined to the *bani* of *Sant* Ravidas only, yet it can be stated that the whole *Bani* is internally dialogical because the *bani* of *Sant* Ravidas toes the thematic lines of the *Guru Granth Sahib.*

NOTES

1. Bani with capital B refers to the whole *Guru Granth Sahib*.
2. "bani" with small b has been referred to the composition of Sant Ravidas in the *Guru Granth Sahib*.
3. Only selected compositions of Sant Ravidas had been incorporated in the Adi Granth by Guru Arjan Dev—the fifth Guru.
4. Since the Bani is an incarnated form of an alive Guru, the Guru is responsive.
5. Ravidas remained monotheistic throughout his life and advocated the concept of a single God which was one of the reasons which prompted Guru Arjan Dev to include his seminal compositions in the *Guru Granth Sahib*.
6. M.A. Macauliffe is considered the first English and non Sikh translator of the *Guru Granth Sahib*. His translation has been used merely to illustrate ideological interactions.
7. The whole *Guru Granth Sahib* is composed in various ragas (musical notations).
8. In modern India the use of the word 'chamaar' is prohibited under the provisions of Indian Constitution and IPC. An address to someone as chamaar is illegal and subject to be penalized.

WORKS CITED

Bakhtin, M.M. "Discourse in the Novel". Trans. Caryl Emerson and Michael Holquist. *The Dialogic Imagination: Four Essays by M.M. Bakhtin.* Ed. Michael Holquist. Austin: University of Texas Press, 1981: 259-422. Google Book Search. Web. 20 Apr. 2009.

——. "Epic and Novel" Trans. Caryl Emerson and Michael Holquist. *The Dialogic Imagination: Four Essays by M.M. Bakhtin*. Ed. Michael Holquist. Austin: University of Texas Press, 1981: 3-40. Google Book Search. Web. 20 Apr. 2009.

——. "From the Prehistory of Novelistic Discourse". Trans. Caryl Emerson and Michael Holquist. *The Dialogic Imagination: Four Essays by M.M. Bakhtin.* Ed. Michael Holquist. Austin: University of Texas Press, 1981: 41-83. Google Book Search. Web. 20 Apr. 2009.

——. *Problems of Dostoevsky's Poetics*. Trans. and ed. Caryl Emerson. Minnesota: University of Minnesota Press, 1984. en.bookfi.org. web. 26 August, 2013.

——. 'The Problem of Speech Genres'. Trans. Vern M. McGee. Speech Genres And Other Late Essays: M.M. Bakhtin. Ed. Caryl Emerson and Michael Holquist Austin: University of Texas Press, 1986. en.bookfi.org. web. 23 Sep. 2009.

Bakhtin, M.M. and P.N. Medvedev. *The Formal Method in Literary Scholarship* (1928). Trans. A.J. Wehrle. Baltimore: Johns Hopkins University Press, 1978. Reprinted in *The Bakhtin Reader: Selected Writings of Bakhtin, Medvedev and Voloshinov*. Ed. Pam Morris. London: Arnold Publishers, 1994. Google Book Search. web. 1 Feb. 2010.

Chatterjee, Chhanda. "Striving for 'Beghampura—the City of No-Sorrow': The Life and Times of Bhagat Ravidas". *The Sikh Review*. 60.12 (2012).

Cole, W. Owen and Piara Singh Sambhi. *The Sikhs: Their Religious Beliefs and Practice.* London; Boston: Routledge and Kegan Paul, 1978. Google Book Search. web. July 2011.

Gerow, Edwin. *Indian Poetics (A History of Indian Literature)*. Wiesbaden: Otto Harrassowitz, 1978.

Giri, Ananta Kumar. "Literature, Society and the Calling of Creative Public Spheres". *Society, Literature and Textuality* ed. Sukalpa Bhattacharjee and C. Joshua Thomas. New Delhi: Sage Publications, 2013: 78-103.

Holquist, Michael. *Dialogism*. London and New York: Routledge, 2002 (second Ed.). Google Book Search. web. 4 May 2005.

Holquist, Michael. Introduction. *The Dialogic Imagination: Four Essays by M.M. Bakhtin.* Ed. Michael Holquist. Trans. Caryl Emerson, and Michael Holquist. Austin: University of Texas Press, 1981. xv-xxxiv. Google Book Search. Web. 20 Apr. 2009.

Homer, Katie. Chaucer's Novelized and Carnivalized Exemplum: A Bakhtinian Reading of the Friar's Tale. *The Chaucer Review*. 45.1 (2010). Penn State University Press. 85-105. Project Muse. web. 7 Nov. 2013.

Kalsi, Sewa Singh. *Religions of the World—Sikhism.* Philadelphia: Chelsea House Publishers, 2005. Google Book Search. web. 7 Mar 2005.

Kohli, Surinder Singh. *Guru Granth Sahib: An Analytical Study*. Amritsar: Singh Brothers, 1961. Reprint. 2005.

Lorenzen, David. Who Invented Hinduism? *Comparative Studies in Society and Religion.* 41.4 (1999). Cambridge University Press. 330-59. JSTOR. Web. 7 Nov. 2013.

Macauliffe, Max Arthur. *The Sikh Religion: Its Gurus, Sacred Writings and Authors*. Vol. 6. Oxford: Clarendon Press, 1909. web. 25 Nov. 2011.

McGee, Vern M. trans. *Speech Genres and Other Late Essays: M.M. Bakhtin*. Ed. Caryl Emerson and Michael Holquist. Austin: University of Texas Press, 1986. en.bookfi.org. Web. 23 Sep. 2009.

McLeod, W.H. *Historical Dictionary of Sikhism.* 2nd ed. Maryland: The Scarecrow Press, 2005. Google Book Search. Web. 23 Nov. 2008.

Schomar, Karine and W.H. McLeod, Ed. *The Sants: Studies in a Devotional Tradition of India.* New Delhi: Jaindra Press, 1987. Google Book Search. Web.

Sen, Amartya. *The Argumentative Indian: Writings on Indian History, Culture and Identity*. New York: Farrar, Straus and Giroux, 2005. Google Book Search. Web. 10 Dec. 2012.

Singh, Daljeet. *Essentials of Sikhism*. Amritsar: Singh Brothers, 1994. http://www.sikhinstitute.org/. Web. 15 July 2013.

——.The Sikh Ideology. Chandigarh: Institute of Sikh Studies, 1997. http://www.sikhinstitute.org/. Web. 15 July 2013.

Singh, Gurbhagat. "Sikhism and Postmodernism". *The Sikh Review*. Nov. 1999. www. sikhreview.org. web. 3 Sep. 2010.

Singh, I.J. "The Nature of Dialogue". *The Sikh Review*. 60.5 (2012): 43-46.

Singh, Khushwant. *A History of the Sikhs (1469-1839)* Vol. 1. New Delhi: Oxford University Press, 2004.

Singh, Pashaura. *The Guru Granth Sahib: Canon, Meaning and Authority*. New Delhi: Oxford University Press, 2000.

Vaudeville, Charllote and Partin, Harry. Kabir and Interior Religion. *History of Religions* 3.2. n.p: The University of Chicago Press, 1964: 191-201. web. 4 Mar 2014.

Winternitz, Maurice. *History of Indian Literature*, Vol. 3. New Delhi: Motilal Banarsidas Publisher, 1999 and 2008. web. Books.google.com.

❑❑❑

Language and Aesthetics in *Hamlet*

RITU SALUJA

ASK even an inexperienced reader and he would not deny the beauty Shakespeare infused in his language while painting his thoughts. The fluidity of an idea melts together with the music of his language and his choice of words rendering his literary oeuvre evergreen and eternal. "I'll make my heaven in a lady's (your) lap" (*Henry VI*, Act 3, Scene 2) gifts the same sensual blushing smile on the face of the beloved today when she hears her man say these lines. Complex but not intelligible, Shakespeare's language offers quotes for all the remotely possible human emotions thus making him English language's most quoted author. It won't be inappropriate if we say that literature is incomplete without William Shakespeare. But what makes the world go gaga over his creations? Or, to put in other words, what is that is bereft in the works of other literati that doesn't match up the level, making Shakespeare an unrivalled and unmatched magic further? The answer is obvious—the beauty he weaves as the pages of his plays run by.

Patricia Parker also favours the use of wise and witty language by Shakespeare and holds the view that Shakespeare's wordplay provided a fertile soil for the growth of the extravagant—and ornamental language neoclassical age is known for. Thus, language of literature also analyses socio-political and contemporary ideology. Parker says that Shakespeare's plays also carried in them the ideology prevalent in the Renaissance. Re-reading of a work helps us concentrate on the undelivered meanings that go unobserved by the audience of a particular social milieu, because of the use of intelligent wordplay. This multiplicity is the basic purpose of language aesthetics. Like Parker, nineteenth-century philosopher Schopenhauer also appreciates the importance of sublime saying that in a tragedy the reader/viewer is exposed to the harsh stony realities of life but at the same time learns that like the protagonist even he can fight that tough battle. All these feelings are expressed only in words, thereby making language ethical.

Shakespeare presents a legion of human emotions which can further be un-layered if we change the eyes we wear. In an attempt to deconstruct his works, we shall explore the subcultures present in *Hamlet*—one of the four great tragedies by William Shakespeare and how the language of Shakespeare performs when seen under the light of Silvan Tomkins's *Affect Theory* and *Script Theory.* When a person is *affected* by some stimulus, event or some memory, s/he experiences some kind of *emotion* as a result. Affects (a noun) are inbuilt and each (set of) affect has its own emotion (result). This ability to 'feel' (awareness about that stimulus) may be switched off by some distraction. In literature—fiction and non-fiction alike—it happens through the language's use.

Donald Nathanson, in *Shame and Pride*, summarises this as "*affect* is biology, *feeling* is psychology and *emotion* is biography."[1] He elaborates that Silvan Tomkins introduced 'Affect Theory' in "Affect Imagery Consciousness" (1962-92) saying that affect is "biological portion of emotion...hard-wired, pre-programmed, genetically transmitted mechanisms that exist in each of us...." Taking this theory ahead and analysing it with the character of Hamlet in Shakespeare's *Hamlet*, we observe the *already present* attributes of sensitivity and morality in him. Hamlet has been shown as a melancholic and a depressed, confused and devastated prince affecting the readers/audience with pity, fear and disgust. The *language Shakespeare uses to arouse the similar feelings in the reader/audience and the function that 'script' does can be judged only if the particular reader/viewer (without any distraction observes the change in his facial contours corresponding to the 'mood' or the stimulus the scene provides.* Silvan Tomkins posited the 'Script Theory' as a step progressive to the maiden 'Affect Theory' and in the 'Script Theory' he suggests that human behaviour has categories and patterns called 'scripts'. These scripts react to an external propelling force thereby affecting the audience or the reader. This constitutes the beauty or aesthetics of the language. Classical writers are generally known to have a very mesmerising enchantment of language making the works classics.

The main emphasis in deconstructing and searching a *subculture* can be pictured upon the women characters that shape up. The ambiguity and suddenness of the thoughts in the main characters are brought forward, with Prince Hamlet putting harsh remarks on the upbringing of the women characters, namely Ophelia and his own mother Gertrude who marries her late husband's murderer and also brother, Claudius. Though it's not certain in the plot of the play that Gertrude had known the cause of her late husband's tragic demise when she married Claudius.

Hamlet again and again pricks and pokes the emotions and feelings of Ophelia, who is set to marry him. In one way or the other, he scrutinizes her values and love for him with rough statements and verses, whereas, he is himself in disguise of the person he's showing himself to be. He acts mad and in the act of madness does break her heart. Other than Hamlet, it is Ophelia's own father, Polonious who uses her as a tool to cast a shadow on Hamlet's plans and in this manner he could spy on him, reducing her as a *subaltern object* abjecting her existence. Polonious wanted to cultivate the meddle, as he formed an ardent liking for drama. Later, he could have travelled the news, to Claudius. In one way, he doesn't care but uses his daughter as an object for his vested interests.

Ophelia has got a lot many reviews "that seldom point towards her innocent disposition and she is plotted as an easy prey to male-chauvinism. Herein the play, an angelic and a whore differentiation comes to score when Ophelia submits herself to her love, through the lines, "I shall obey my lord" (Act 1, Scene 3, line 126). Hamlet accuses her father by continuing his tempestuous pronunciation that, "You are a fishmonger" (Act 2, Scene 2, line 174), referring to his daughter. Jacqueline Rose has pinpointed the misogynist elements in Hamlet's character. The societal perception of that time is well underpinned, with the two expectations from the women—one of chastity and an unquestioning surrender to male-chauvinistic repressive forces. This numbs Ophelia's senses blurring the ravine between the right and the wrong. She submits to Hamlet's vices of manners by not answering him or confronting his obligations. Ophelia paints the Renaissance women as submissive and weak who shall only succumb as to not answer for the discomfort ushered upon them. Then there is Gertrude—the 'frail woman'. Whereas her marriage with Claudius need not be only to fulfil her physical needs and she can't be only regarded as someone, who was fully dependent on the new King. Being espoused to Claudius, she never treated with disregard and never lost the remembrance of her womb being evenly umbrelling the fact of her Queenhood—the political responsibilities that fluttered on her shoulders—Denmark. Gertrude patted her son, "Good Hamlet, cast thy nightly colour off/ And let thine eye look like a friend on Denmark" (Act 1, Scene 2, line 70). She celebrated Hamlet's martial dexterous prowess to the extent of disobeying her husband. She did drink the poison accidentally, kicking the bucket and feathering the tragic genre of the play. Gertrude became a sufferer, caught between the fierce relation of her beloved son and her husband. Both the women's silence absorbed the socially pervasive marginality forming a Renaissance sub-culture. The idea of "perverse dynamic" which happens to be a very informative theoretical concept that was first talked about in Sexual Dissidence (Dollimore, 1991), says that this 'dynamic' breathes in the society itself. It turns out not to be a remote 'alien thing' as it is supposed to be, rather it enables a tracking-back of the 'other' into the 'same'. Thus, the 'other' is around the 'centre' always. About this Dollimore speaks of his analysis of one of Shakespeare's play pointing out how the 'absence' of an element in the margin draws the same margin into limelight. They are made (in the words of Barbara Babcock) 'symbolically central' even while remaining utterly marginal: everything in the play presupposes them, yet they have no voice or presence. Mouth-cuffed existence of these 'margins' is a loud iteration of their vulnerability and power-depleted status. Their existential muting caught the attention of the New Historicists and Cultural Materialists later in the mid-1980s. If New Historicism and Cultural Materialism are the methodologies that study those who are at the margins, then Dollimore is correct when he claims that most imperative issues of existence and representation, literature's and discourse's relation to it, the im/possibility of searching and recovering the history of these muted exclusions and an all-pervasive margins, social reception vis-à-vis gender needs to be now looked back in retrospect. Generally referred to as a 'weak queen', Gertrude's 'weakness' lied in her gender—her socially constructed identity and her hamartia became her incessant unfulfilled desire to be loved. This has attracted a huge criticism and an alarming attention of the feminist critics always. Claudius who's more at fault is not hit with any gender remarks as "Frailty, thy name is woman..." (Act 1, Scene 2, line 147). If the claim of 'being a man' is what Hamlet reiterates, we all nod when one claims that master-minding the death of King Hamlet made Claudius no 'man' for frailty lied in the very character of Claudius. Wasn't the 'fact' of being the 'man' called for Hamlet's probing into the matter and learning that Gertrude was too, carried away victimised in Claudius's lust for power? Doesn't Gertrude become a mere 'stepping-stone' and an 'object' used to catapult Claudius to power?

Both the women's tragic consequence to their desire to be loved forms a feminist sub-cultural reading of the text where in the major plot of power, treachery and in/justice, the 'minor other' is rendered unattended longing for love and respect—both Gertrude and Ophelia. Margaret Atwood in her collection of short stories, *Good Bones* (O.W. Toad, 1992) writes '*Gertrude Talks Back*' where she rewrites the famous closet scene in Shakespeare's tragedy *Hamlet* making Gertrude retaliate the "Frailty, thy name is woman" notion. When Hamlet finally determines to make her see the ghastly error of her choice, his cruelly-chosen words force her to feel guilty. The language's 'Affect' is seen in the eyes of the audience/readers with a forehead frowned in pity and sympathy making them feel the aesthetic beauty of words and their effect.

O Hamlet, speak no more
Thou turn'st mine eyes into my very soul,
And there I see such black and grained spots
As will not leave their tinct.[2]

Franco Zeffirelli in his 1990 film adaptation of the play *Hamlet*, stages the scene with Gertrude and Claudius (played by Glenn Close and Alan Bates, respectively) in such a way that Gertrude always appears to be looking over Claudius' shoulder. The scene has been charged aesthetically and what grips the audience is the womb-vermillion clash which she is unable to decipher. She is trying hard to analyse her relation (and Claudius's) with her son. Thus, Gertrude is seen throughout as a mother who is trying to reconfigure her family around her new husband Claudius. She also assumes a new responsibility to paint the verbal portrait of Ophelia's death and to deliver an elegy for her would be daughter in law on her death.

Sweets to the sweet! Farewell, [Scatters flowers]
I hoped thou shouldst have been my Hamlet's wife.
I thought thy bride bed to have decked, sweet maid,
And not have, strewed thy grave.[3]

Gertrude's love for Hamlet and her liking for Ophelia as her prospective daughter in law are shown through her behaviour and the few dialogues Shakespeare has dedicated in this respect. Again, behaviour is the only evidence we have with respect to Gertrude's guilt. In Scene 5 of Act 1, where the ghost reveals the treacherous murder of King Hamlet—"the serpent that did sting thy father's life now wears his crown..." it remains silent about Gertrude's involvement with it and being physically present in the garden. Readers misread "...that adulterate beast..." (Act 1, Scene 5, 42-45) by interpreting Gertrude's sexual involvement with Claudius before King Hamlet's death. Whereas it is also interpreted otherwise by some critics—"If Gertrude were an adulteress, she would have been almost certainly been involved in Claudius' plot of murder, and therefore she would be the play's villainess and not its child-like victim. Claudius would believe her to be an accomplice and confide in her, but he does not. Moreover, if it were true, it most surely would be foremost on Hamlet's mind, but when Hamlet confronts Gertrude in her closet and announces all her crimes, he does not once even imply that she has committed adultery".[4] This 'trace' (a Derridian concept) is what forms the aesthetical value of a text or/and its characters. The beauty lies in analysing "mark(s) of the absence of a presence, an always-already absent present", that seems to be "the condition of thought and experience" as "language bears within itself the necessity of its own critique".[5]

Recent studies and researches in the humanities, which can be grouped under the common label of 'post-structuralist theory,' have done a lottowards making us sensitive to the politics of culture, in general, and of literature, in particular. Much critical ink has been spilled over the last few decades on how the literary canon originates and holds its ground, and on the relations between canonical and non-canonical and also between the centre and the margins. A well-known post-colonial theorist and philosopher Edward Said explains—"power to narrate, or to block other narratives from forming and emerging, is very important to culture and imperialism, and constitutes one of the main connections between them".[6] "Here as in other respects, the political agendas of feminism and post-colonialism overlap; both aim at challenging the canon and at inscribing the experiences of the marginal subject (female and/or post-colonial)".[7] T.S. Eliot, in his famous essay "Hamlet and his Problems" opines that the major reason why Hamlet is dejected and devastated is Gertrude's sinful behaviour. He states, "Shakespeare's Hamlet...is a play dealing with the effect of a mother's guilt upon her son".[8] This free interpretation of Shakespeare's language in *Hamlet* grasps the 'aesthetical value' which is the centre around which this paper is aimed.

NOTES

1. Nathanson, Donald L. (1992), *Shame and Pride: Affect, Sex, and the Birth of the Self* (Chapter 2), New York: WAV. Norton.

2. Shakespeare, William. Hamlet. Routledge, New Delhi. PB. Act 111, Scene iv, pp. 88-91.
3. Fraility, Thy name is woman: Gertrude: in the middle. Web.
4. Introduction to Gertrude in *Hamlet.* Web. www.shakespeare-online.com/plays/hamlet/gertrudecharacter.html
5. Macksey, Richard and Donato, Eugenio (ed.). *The Languages of Criticism and The Sciences of Man: The Structuralist Controversy* (Baltimore, 1970), p. 254.
6. Diffley, Kathleen (ed.). *Witness to Reconstruction: Constance Fenimore Woolson and the Postbellum South, 1873-1874*, p. 61.
7. Dominguez, Pilar Cuder. Rewriting Canonical Portrayals of Women: Margaret Atwood's *Gertrude Talks Back.* Web. www.literature-study-online.com essays/atwood-gertrudehtml elsinore.ucsc.edu/women/womenGertrude.html
8. "Hamlet and His Problems". *The Sacred Wood: Essays on Poetry and Criticism*, 1922.

❑❑❑